Greenhouse Gardening for Beginners

The Complete Guide to Building Your Own Greenhouse and Growing Organic Vegetables, Fruits, Herbs, and Flowers Year-Round

Max Barnes

© COPYRIGHT 2024 MAX BARNES - ALL RIGHTS RESERVED.

The content contained within this book may not be reproduced, duplicated or transmitted without direct written permission from the author or the publisher.

Under no circumstances will any blame or legal responsibility be held against the publisher, or author, for any damages, reparation, or monetary loss due to the information contained within this book. Either directly or indirectly.

Legal Notice:

This book is copyright protected. This book is only for personal use. You cannot amend, distribute, sell, use, quote or paraphrase any part, or the content within this book, without the consent of the author or publisher.

Disclaimer Notice:

Please note the information contained within this document is for educational and entertainment purposes only. All effort has been executed to present accurate, up to date, and reliable, complete information. No warranties of any kind are declared or implied. Readers acknowledge that the author is not engaging in the rendering of legal, financial, medical or professional advice. The content within this book has been derived from various sources. Please consult a licensed professional before attempting any techniques outlined in this book.

By reading this document, the reader agrees that under no circumstances is the author responsible for any losses, direct or indirect, which are incurred as a result of the use of the information contained within this document, including, but not limited to, — errors, omissions, or inaccuracies.

Your Free Gift

I'd like to offer you a gift as a way of saying thank you for purchasing this book. It's the eBook called 5 Easy Ways to Preserve Your Harvest. Sooner or later, you'll reach a point where you're able to grow more vegetables and fruits than you can eat, so I've created this book to help you preserve your harvest so that you could enjoy it later. You can get your free eBook by scanning the QR code below with your phone camera and joining our community. Alternatively, please send me an email to **maxbarnesbooks@gmail.com** and I will send you the free eBook.

SPECIAL BONUS!

Want this book for free?

Get FREE unlimited access to it and all of my new books by joining our community!

Scan with your phone camera to join!

Garden Planner, Journal and Log Book

Keeping a journal to keep track of your garden and plants can help you determine what worked well and what didn't so that you can repeat your successes and avoid mistakes in the future. To help you plan your garden as well as keep all the important information about your garden and plants in one convenient place in an organized manner, I've created a garden planner, journal, and log book. Please scan the QR code below to find out more. Alternatively, please send me an email to **maxbarnesbooks@gmail.com** and I will send you the link to the journal.

Scan with your phone camera to find out more

Contents

Introduction 7
    What This Book Will Cover 7
    Why I'm Writing This Book 7

Chapter 1: Choosing the Right Greenhouse for You 9
    What is a Greenhouse and How Does it Work? 9
    Types of Greenhouses 9
    Types of Greenhouse Materials 14
    Considerations for Choosing Your Greenhouse .. 18
    Greenhouse Building Permit 20

Chapter 2: Planning and Building Your Greenhouse 23
    Planning Your Greenhouse 23
    Building Your Greenhouse 29

Chapter 3: Greenhouse Environment 35
    Temperature 35
    Humidity 38
    Light 39
    Greenhouse Seasons 40

Chapter 4: Soil—Creating the Perfect Growing Medium 43
    Gardening Tools 43
    Preparing Garden Beds 45
    Building Raised Beds 48
    Checking and Changing Soil pH Level 51

Chapter 5: Seeding and Transplanting .. 53
    Selecting and Starting Seeds 53
    Growing and Transplanting Seedlings 57
    Propagating Plants from Cuttings 60
    Maximizing Growing Space 61

Chapter 6: Maintaining Your Greenhouse Garden 65
    Watering 65
    Mulching 67
    Managing Weeds In and Around the Greenhouse 69
    Fertilizing 70
    Compost 72
    General Garden Care and Maintenance 74
    Greenhouse Maintenance and Cleaning 79

Chapter 7: Pest Control and Dealing with Diseases 82
    Common Garden Pests 82
    Organic Pest Control Methods 89
    Dealing with Diseases 93
    Disease Prevention 101
    Crop Rotation 102
    Companion Planting for Disease Management .. 104

Chapter 8: Time to Harvest the Bounty 106
    When and How to Harvest Your Vegetables 106
    Storing Your Harvest 110

Chapter 9: Plant Profiles 114
    Vegetables 114
    Fruits 124
    Herbs 125
    Flowers 128

Conclusion 131

Resources 132

Index 136

Introduction

You may be wondering what is so wonderful about greenhouse gardening? The main advantage of greenhouses is that they allow you to create the perfect growing conditions for your plants, which means that potentially you could grow delicious vegetables, fruits, and herbs year-round. There is a great variety of greenhouses, from cold frames to hoop houses to massive framed structures. Some of them work as season extenders, but others can be used to grow plants year-round. It seems incredible to believe you could grow fresh, delicious vegetables year-round. But it's true, and this book will help you learn how to do it with ease and effectively.

Many people want to grow their own food in a greenhouse, but they're often unsure about where to start. Beginners can feel overwhelmed when they think about greenhouse gardening and assume it's too complicated because they either don't have the knowledge about gardening or they mistrust the information they find online because it has conflicting information and doesn't look like it's from a reputable, quality source. This book will teach beginners to greenhouse gardening everything they need to know about choosing and building a greenhouse, starting their own garden, and growing vegetables organically and efficiently year-round.

What This Book Will Cover

Chapter 1 will cover different types of greenhouses available and help you choose the perfect one for your needs.

Chapter 2 will help you plan and build your greenhouse, including everything from choosing the perfect location to planning the actual greenhouse inside and out and finally building it.

Chapter 3 is all about controlling the greenhouse environment to create the perfect growing conditions for your plants, including adjusting temperature, humidity, and light. This chapter also covers which plants are best to grow during different seasons.

Chapter 4 is all about preparing the soil, starting garden beds using the no-dig method, and building raised beds if you'd prefer to go that route.

Chapter 5 will look at starting seeds and transplanting seedlings. It will also cover propagating plants from cuttings.

Chapter 6 will cover everything you need to know about maintaining your garden and greenhouse, looking at watering, mulching, weeding, general garden maintenance and care as well as greenhouse cleaning and maintenance.

Chapter 7 will cover pest control and dealing with diseases using organic options as well as disease prevention.

Chapter 8 will let you know the best time to harvest your vegetables, fruits, and herbs and provide information on how to store them.

Chapter 9 contains plant profiles that provide detailed information on how to grow various vegetables, fruits, herbs, and flowers. This is intended as a useful reference resource for you to refer back to when required.

Why I'm Writing This Book

My name is Max. I grew up on a farm as a child, and helping my grandmother Anna with her garden is one of my earliest childhood memories. My grandmother was very much ahead of her time and was very innovative. She experimented with different gardening methods, and I learned from this and continued to do this myself all throughout my adult life. I grow the majority of vegetables, fruits, and herbs we eat on my property using different methods, including growing in greenhouses. Greenhouse gardening helps me live a sustainable lifestyle and grow plants year-round.

When I'm in my garden, it always brings back fond childhood memories of helping my grandmother on her farm. I learned so much about gardening in general, and greenhouse gardening in particular, from my grandmother. Throughout my adult life and up until this day, I have continued to keep my knowledge up-to-date, and I keep experimenting with different gardening methods so that I am able to grow a variety of plants all year round—lovely, delicious organic vegetables, fruits, and herbs that make our mealtimes a delight!

I am enthusiastic about gardening, and greenhouse gardening in particular, because it has so many incredible benefits. I want to show people that greenhouse gardening is not difficult, and that the benefits of doing it far outweigh the time, money, and effort invested. It will get you fresh, delicious crops year-round, and it will help you live a healthier and more sustainable lifestyle.

I've learned a lot from my grandmother. I've kept a garden all my life, and it's been key to the sustainable lifestyle we live. I want to share my knowledge on how to live more sustainably with others who have an interest in it. Over the years, I've learned a lot: what not to do and pitfalls to avoid and things that are good to do that can help reap great benefits. I'd like to help people avoid the mistakes I've made and get there a little quicker using the helpful tips, tricks, and techniques I've come across during all the years I've been keeping a garden. I've had a lot of help with greenhouse gardening from my grandmother as well as my friends and colleagues from whom I've learned over the years, and I'd like to give back and share some of that knowledge.

This book is a guide to growing organic vegetables, fruits, and herbs in greenhouses. It is not a guide to anything else outside the realm of greenhouse gardening and vegetable gardening in general.

Without further ado, let's jump into Chapter 1 and learn all about different types of greenhouses so that you can choose the perfect one for your needs.

Chapter 1: Choosing the Right Greenhouse for You

You're probably excited to build your greenhouse and start growing fresh, delicious produce year-round, but you might be wondering what kind of greenhouse you should get, especially considering there are so many different types available. Not to worry—in this chapter, you'll learn how greenhouses actually work, what different types of greenhouses are available, the types of materials used to build greenhouses, and finally, how to choose the perfect greenhouse for you. So, without further ado, let's get right into it!

What is a Greenhouse and How Does it Work?

If someone asked you what a greenhouse is, you would likely say it's a structure with glass walls and roof used to grow plants year-round, and you would be totally right. However, I think it would be beneficial to explain what exactly greenhouses are and how they work first.

Simply put, a greenhouse is a glass- or plastic-enclosed framed structure that is designed to regulate the temperature and humidity of the environment inside, which allows you to grow plants year-round in most climates.

Greenhouses can also be called glasshouses or hothouses, and these terms are often used interchangeably; however, there are subtle differences between them. Greenhouses can be constructed with a variety of materials, such as wood and plastic. A glasshouse, on the other hand, is a traditional type of greenhouse made only of glass panes that allow light to enter. Hothouses are essentially greenhouses that are artificially heated. However, both heated and unheated structures can generally be classified as greenhouses.

With that out of the way, let's take a look at how greenhouses actually work. In short, greenhouses work by converting light energy into heat. Since they have glass or plastic sheeting, it allows sunlight to enter the greenhouse, where it heats up everything inside the greenhouse. The walls of a greenhouse help keep the heat in. Greenhouses can get too hot sometimes, so you'll need to have vents and fans to prevent the plants inside of your greenhouse from overheating.

Greenhouses serve as a shield between nature and what you are growing, and they allow growing seasons to be extended as well as possibly improved. They also provide shelter from excess cold or heat as well as pests.

The main benefit of having a greenhouse is the growing environment inside the greenhouse can be controlled, which allows you to create the perfect growing conditions for your plants. You can control the light that comes in, the temperature, and the moisture in the air. Greenhouses don't have many disadvantages apart from the fact that they can be a bit costly to build; however, I personally think they are worth every penny.

So, now that you know what exactly greenhouses are and how they work, let's take a look at different types of greenhouses as well as their pros and cons.

Types of Greenhouses

Greenhouse styles can vary from attached to freestanding structures that vary in shape and design. Attached styles include lean-to and abutting, and freestanding greenhouses include gable-style, A-frame, gothic arch, geodesic dome, as well as hoop house (Quonset) styles. Let's take a closer look at each of these types of greenhouses and their pros and cons.

Attached Greenhouses

Attached greenhouses are typically placed against a side of a building or attached to one side of an existing structure, hence the name. Attached greenhouses include lean-to and abutting styles.

Lean-To

Lean-to greenhouses are built onto the wall of an existing structure and slope away from it, preferably southerly. This simple design is ideal for urban properties with limited space. Even though the side facing the building is dark, the heat radiating from the building warms the greenhouse, plus the building adds stability.

Most lean-to types of greenhouses don't exceed 12 feet (4 m) and can only carry one or two rows of plants at a time. However, you can extend it against a longer wall, while ensuring it gets ample sunlight.

Pros

- Requires little space to set up
- Cheap to build and maintain
- Fewer support requirements for the roof
- Near to amenities like electricity and water from the main building

Cons

- Provides limited space for plants
- Has limited light exposure because it's attached to a wall
- Hard to control the temperature because of the wall sides
- Height limitation due to the supporting wall

Abutting

Abutting greenhouses are similar to lean-to—they also attach to an existing structure. The difference is that the building the greenhouse is attached to forms the end of the greenhouse, and not a side wall—the greenhouse is perpendicular to the building and the roof slopes to either side. When built in front of a door, the greenhouse can make a nice sunroom.[1]

Pros

- Can help reduce heating costs during colder months, as the greenhouse acts as a buffer zone that absorbs and radiates warmth
- Easier and cheaper to build compared to freestanding greenhouses since they use existing house walls and only three sides typically need to be constructed
- By connecting the greenhouse to your home, you are effectively using what might otherwise be a waste of space

Cons

- Limited space—attached greenhouses are typically smaller than freestanding ones
- Less sun exposure because it's attached to a wall
- Designing an attached greenhouse that is both functional and looks aesthetically pleasing can be a challenge
- If the existing house foundation can't support the weight of the greenhouse, structural modifications or a separate foundation may be required
- Permit may be required for construction depending on local regulations and building codes

Freestanding Greenhouses

Freestanding greenhouses can have different shapes, and these include gable-style, A-frame, gothic arch, hoop house (Quonset), and geodesic dome shapes. This type of structure is what you would likely envision when the word "greenhouse" is mentioned.

A freestanding greenhouse is usually the best choice if you have the space and money to build one.

One advantage of a freestanding greenhouse is that it's easier to achieve and maintain different temperatures to meet specific crop requirements. In addition, the light in a freestanding greenhouse is uniformly distributed over the entire growing area. Furthermore, freestanding greenhouses are easier to ventilate without exposing plants to erratic temperature fluctuations or harsh blasts of cold air. With that said, let's take a closer look at different types of freestanding greenhouses.

Gable-Style Greenhouses

Gable-style greenhouses have flat, sloping roofs connected to vertical sidewalls. The roof angle determines how well snow slides off as well as the total height of the greenhouse. This type of greenhouse design can use either glass or rigid plastic panels. This is perhaps the most common design and is something that would typically come to mind when you think of a greenhouse. Gable-style greenhouses are easy to build, provide plenty of sunlight to plants inside, and have ample room to move inside.

---

[1] Image from https://www.flickr.com/photos/hartleybotanic/14821857123

Pros

- Uncomplicated design and easy to build
- Maximizes interior space due to its simple shape with vertical walls
- Efficient air circulation, especially alongside walls

Cons

- Requires more materials (wood and metal) than some other designs

A-Frame Greenhouses

A-frame greenhouses are similar to gable-style and are even easier to build. They have a basic triangular design with long, sloped roofs that extend all the way to the ground. These greenhouses are usually made of glass or polycarbonate panels. A-frame greenhouses maximize light, but space and airflow are limited underneath the parts of the roof close to the ground.[2]

Pros

- Easy to build
- Low construction costs

Cons

- Not as space efficient as other designs due to its shape

---

[2] Image from https://www.bobvila.com/articles/diy-greenhouse-plans/

Gothic Arch Greenhouses

Gothic arch greenhouses are somewhat of a hybrid of gable-style and A-frame designs. The frame is made with aluminum, steel, or PVC poles that curve gracefully to join with a ridge cap and form a pointed roof, reminiscent of an old gothic cathedral (hence the name). The curved shape means there's no need for structural trusses, which can help you save on building costs. It's a strong structure that easily sheds snow and rain, but it limits interior side wall headroom and space. It's easy to build and is arguably the most elegant type of greenhouse. Due to the curved walls, you would need a flexible material, such as polycarbonate film.

Pros

- A good compromise of construction costs and interior space between gable-style and A-frame designs
- Fewer supports needed than some other designs, which can help save on construction costs
- Sheds snow and water easily due to its shape

Cons

- Some loss of interior space due to its shape compared to gable-style designs, but it's still considerably roomier than A-frame designs

Hoop House (Quonset) Greenhouses

These greenhouses are constructed from a series of semi-circular hoops. They are cheap and really easy to build—you just need to attach the ends of the hoops to base plates or stick them into the ground, and they automatically form the supports for the walls and roof.

This type of greenhouse is ideal for covering long rows, and they provide more room near the walls than A-frame structures. They must be covered with something flexible, like polycarbonate film or insect netting depending on the season. One of their drawbacks is that they don't shed snow and water as well as other structures. If you live in an area with heavy snowfall or stormy weather, you will need to reinforce your hoop house. They are not as sturdy as other designs, but they are very affordable and easy to ventilate.[3]

Pros

- Very affordable
- Easy to build
- Easy to ventilate

Cons

- Not as sturdy as other designs
- Wind can be a problem if the sheeting is not correctly installed

Geodesic Dome Greenhouses

These greenhouses look incredibly cool and futuristic, like something straight out of a sci-fi movie. However, they are easier to build than you might think, and they are incredibly strong, energy efficient, and hold up well in severe weather conditions. Their intricate design helps maximize light transmission for plants and also makes it easy to install vents, which helps promote adequate airflow. However, due to their unconventional shape, it might be challenging to arrange plants in an organized way inside.

You can make your own frame by making sticks or rods of the same length and assembling them with connectors in a series of triangles. But I would recommend purchasing a kit that includes everything you need. Even so, they are more difficult to assemble than other structures.[4]

---

[3] Image from https://www.almanac.com/how-to-build-hoop-house

[4] Image from https://www.snowdondomes.com/portfolio/shirleys-domes-35m-diameter-polycarbonate-dome

Pros

- Very durable
- Great light transmission
- Unique look

Cons

- Can be difficult to build

Cold Frames

A cold frame is essentially a miniature greenhouse—it's a cover made with glass or plastic that you place over your garden beds. It helps extend the growing season and protect your plants from frost, low temperatures, rain, snow, and wind. One thing to note with cold frames is that you have to watch your plants carefully and open the frame up when needed because otherwise your plants might get overheated quite easily.[5]

Pros

- Very easy to build
- Cheap

Cons

- Overheating can be a problem

Types of Greenhouse Materials

Whether you want to build a small greenhouse for just a few of your favorite plants or a huge one that will allow you to grow an abundance of vegetables year-round, choosing the right greenhouse materials for your needs is key to having a bountiful harvest. Not so long ago, greenhouses were mostly used by commercial plant producers who require a protected, controlled environment to grow food crops and flowers off-season or to raise starter plants and shrubs for sale. However, more recently, with the new modern materials and new construction techniques, greenhouses have become available to anyone interested in gardening. In fact, it's quite common today to see small greenhouses in residential backyards.

Greenhouse frames, coverings, and flooring can be made from a combination of materials, each changing the effectiveness of your greenhouse, so it's important to use the right building materials for your greenhouse so that your plants can thrive in it. All the different greenhouse materials have different structures and panel types they work best with. Let's take a look at different greenhouse materials available and their pros and cons so that you can choose the materials that would work best for your specific needs.

Frame Materials

The frame provides structural integrity and serves to anchor the greenhouse covering. Greenhouse frames are available in a variety of materials, such as aluminum, steel, plastic, and wood.

---

[5] Image from https://www.theplasticpeople.co.uk/advice/blog/march-2022/cold-frame-gardening-for-beginners/

Aluminum

Aluminum frames are strong, lightweight, and will not rust. It is perhaps the most widely used material for greenhouse frames, and it has a very long lifespan. Aluminum frames usually have extruded channels that provide a perfect fit for inserting covering panels. Aluminum is not an insulative material, however, so there will be some heat loss through the frame. Aluminum frames can be powder coated, which further increases their durability and gives you some nice color options.

Steel

Galvanized steel frames are extremely strong, long lasting, and affordable. They usually come in tubular shape. Since steel is really strong, minimal structure is required for framing, which means your plants will get more light. Steel frames are usually covered with polyethylene film because other covering materials require fastening systems that don't work well with steel frameworks. Steel frames are heavy, which helps the greenhouse remain stable in windy conditions, but it also makes transporting and assembling the greenhouse more difficult. Steel is typically used for large commercial greenhouses.

Plastic

Plastic frames are quite popular because they are attractive, less expensive than aluminum, and have less heat loss than aluminum or steel frames. However, they lack the strength of metal frames, so they are mostly used for smaller greenhouses. Plastic frames are typically used with polycarbonate panels.

Wood

Wood frames are commonly used in DIY greenhouse building projects. Wood frames have an aesthetically pleasing appearance and sufficient strength and durability. However, they are susceptible to rot, so it's important to ensure that the wood does not contact the ground or any moisture holding surfaces.

Covering/Glazing Materials

Materials used for outer covering or glazing of greenhouses have come a long way since the old-fashioned glass greenhouses. Nowadays, different types of plastic and tempered glass are used for building applications. They come in the form of sheets or panels and range in clarity from clear to diffused (opaque).

Glass and clear plastic function in essentially the same way—they allow light to pass through while trapping heat inside. Plastics are generally lighter and less expensive but not as durable and weather-resistant as glass. Glass panels are more expensive but hold up better over time.

When choosing covering materials, you should consider whether you want it as a season extender or if you intend to grow plants year-round. If you live in a climate with cold winters, you'll need well-insulated covering. Now let's take a look at different covering materials available as well as their pros and cons.

Tempered Glass

Tempered glass panes are very strong and impact-resistant and will withstand expansion and contraction during seasonal temperature changes. Single-pane thickness of ⅛ inch (3 mm) is adequate for greenhouses, but 5/32 inch (4 mm) thickness is stronger and provides additional insulation. The edges must be protected during installation, as the pane can shatter if hit with a hard object. Tempered glass is more expensive than polycarbonate panels, but it is more durable and scratch-resistant. Tempered glass is clear and provides no diffusion.

Fiberglass

Fiberglass panels are translucent and provide well-diffused light. They retain heat more efficiently than glass. Fiberglass greenhouses are usually corrugated to provide rigidity. Fiberglass panels have outer gel coating on them, which will become sun baked with time, often within 6–10 years depending on exposure. The surface will become etched and yellowed, and dirt and debris can collect in the valleys.

Polycarbonate

Polycarbonate is a modern, high-quality covering material for greenhouses. It's durable, lightweight, and UV-treated. Polycarbonate panels have a relatively long lifespan of 15 years or longer in most regions. They are available in different thicknesses. They provide the clarity of glass but are not as strong or scratch resistant.

Single-walled polycarbonate panels lack the heat retention and strength of multi-walled panels, and they also provide no light diffusion. Twin-walled panels are very popular because they have internal air pockets, which provide added strength and insulation. They also provide diffused light. Triple-walled panels have all the benefits of twin-walled ones, but they are even stronger and have better insulation, which is especially useful in cold climates for year-round gardening. Triple-walled panels will withstand heavy snow loads and freezing without cracking or becoming distorted.

Polyethylene Film

Polyethylene film is commonly used in large commercial greenhouses because it is relatively inexpensive and easy to maintain, plus it's UV treated. It provides semi-diffused light and retains heat well. Polyethylene film only lasts 3–5 years and can stretch or sag in windy conditions or after being loaded with snow. It's also not the most durable material, and it can be poked through by falling branches or torn during winds if not well secured. Polyethylene film is also available in twin-walled version, which has better insulation than single-walled film.

Panel Clarity

Greenhouse panels can be either clear (translucent) or opaque (diffused), and both of these have their own advantages and disadvantages. Some greenhouse can have semi-opaque covers which provide some of the benefits of both clear and opaque panels.

Clear panels provide direct light, while opaque panels provide diffused light. If you want a greenhouse to germinate seeds and grow seedlings that will be later transplanted outdoors, then clear coverings have the advantage of bringing full, direct light. This helps warm the soil and encourage seed germination.

If you plan to grow plants to maturity in your greenhouse, opaque coverings have the advantage of providing even light for balanced foliage growth as well as preventing hot spots within the greenhouse. While it may seem counterintuitive, diffused light is better for growing plants. Although it may appear to be less bright than direct light, diffused light reaches your plants from many angles, so your plants won't get leggy as they would when competing with each other to grow towards available light. With diffused lighting, plants develop a more balanced, compact structure.

If you want a dual-use greenhouse, semi-opaque coverings provide the benefits of both clear and opaque coverings. Semi-opaque panels allow enough direct light for starting seeds, and once the seedlings have been set out, the greenhouse can then be used to grow full-term crops inside. Some greenhouse designs have diffused covering on the roof and clear covering on the sides, which offers some benefits of each.

Insulation

The amount of insulation required for your greenhouse will depend on the climate you live in and whether you want your greenhouse as a season extender or to grow vegetables year-round. Different covering materials offer different degrees of insulation based on their inherent properties. Below you will find a chart showing the relative differences in insulating and heat loss value for greenhouse coverings. R-value is the measurement of insulating ability of the material. Higher R-value refers to higher insulation value. U-value is the measurement of heat loss through the material. The lower the U-value, the less heat is escaping.

Covering material	R-value	U-value
Polyethylene film, single layer	0.83	1.20
⅛ inch (3 mm) single pane glass	0.95	1.05
5/32 inch (4 mm) double wall polycarbonate	1.43	0.70
15/64 inch (6 mm) double wall polycarbonate	1.54	0.65
5/16 inch (8 mm) double wall polycarbonate	1.60	0.63
25/64 inch (10 mm) double wall polycarbonate	1.89	0.53
Double pane storm windows	2.00	0.50
5/16 inch (8 mm) triple wall polycarbonate	2.00	0.50
9/64 inch (3.5 mm) twin-wall polyethylene	2.10	0.48
13/64 inch (5 mm) twin-wall polyethylene	2.30	0.43

Flooring

Greenhouses don't usually need a finished floor, as most of a greenhouse footprint is used as a planting area, which means a level finished surface is not necessary. When choosing your greenhouse flooring, you will first need to decide how you want to grow in the greenhouse—directly in the soil, in raised beds, in containers, or in a hydroponic system. This book will cover growing plants in the soil and raised beds; however, if you're interested in container gardening or hydroponic gardening, I have books dedicated to those topics called *Container Gardening for Beginners* and *Hydroponics for Beginners* respectively, which you can find on Amazon. Let's go over the different types of greenhouse flooring so that you can decide which option is best for you.

Soil Floor

If you'd like to grow directly in the soil, your greenhouse won't have a floor. You can use materials like pavers, flagstone, gravel, or wood planks to create paths between garden beds if needed. You can also mulch your garden beds and paths, which will help prevent weeds, keep the moisture in, keep the soil warm when it's cold and make it cooler when it's hot, and also enrich the soil if you're using organic mulch. Mulching will be covered in detail in Chapter 6.

Having a soil floor and growing directly in the soil offers several benefits. First of all, you can save time and money, as you won't have to finish the floor of your greenhouse. Having a soil floor also promotes healthier root development and enhances the overall vitality of the plants since plants can access the nutrients deep in the soil. Furthermore, growing directly in the soil eliminates the need for containers and potting soil, which can save both time and money. It also enables better water drainage, preventing the risk of waterlogged roots and potential diseases. Moreover, the soil acts as a thermal mass (especially with the insulated foundation), which helps regulate temperature fluctuations within the greenhouse, and this can be beneficial for maintaining optimal growing conditions.

Stone, Pavers, or Gravel Floors

Finishing your greenhouse floor with stone, pavers, or gravel are quite popular options because they work well with raised beds. If you decide to grow in raised beds, I would suggest building raised beds with no flooring material beneath the beds so that they connect directly to the soil. This way, plants' root systems can grow deeper into the soil, which will help them get more nutrients and thrive. You can then make paths between raised beds out of pavers, flagstone, or crushed gravel.

Concrete Floors

Another option is concrete slab flooring. This is a more popular option when growing in containers, hydroponic systems, or self-wicking beds. Concrete floors are expensive, but they have a number of advantages. Concrete slab can act as a foundation for your greenhouse. It's also easy to wash down with a hose. Having concrete floors makes it easy to move growing beds or tables, especially if they are on wheels. Wheelbarrows are also easier to handle on concrete. And finally, concrete provides additional thermal mass, which helps stabilize temperatures in the greenhouse.

Considerations for Choosing Your Greenhouse

With so many different options available, you're probably wondering what type of greenhouse would suit your needs best. So, this section will cover important things you need to consider when choosing a greenhouse so that you can choose the perfect greenhouse for your needs.

Gardening Needs

One of the most important things to consider when choosing a greenhouse is what you actually need it for. Do you want to use it for starting seeds, as a season extender, or to grow plants year-round? For starting seeds, a small greenhouse would be sufficient, preferably with clear covering. If you want a season extender, you could actually get away with using cold frames. However, it you want a proper greenhouse, then you would need a larger one, preferably with opaque or semi-opaque covering. And if you want to grow plants year-round, you'd want a large greenhouse with opaque or semi-opaque covering.

Greenhouse Kits vs Building Your Own Greenhouse

There are a lot of different greenhouse kits available; however, you can build your own greenhouse from the ground up if you want. A lot of people think they can build their own greenhouse at a lower cost than buying a kit, but this is not necessarily true. If you get a standard kit, then it can be cheaper in some cases than buying all the necessary materials separately. However, when you get into customized units, then the cost will go up considerably, plus customizing a kit can be more expensive than building your own greenhouse.

If you have some recycled materials, like wood and glass, then building your own greenhouse can help you save some costs, especially if you're good at DIY and can do it yourself. If you're using recycled glass, make sure it's tempered. If it breaks, it will crinkle and won't cut you. To check whether glass is tempered, you can look in the corners of the glass panes and see if there are "tempered" or "temp" markings in one of the corners.

Space

Another important consideration is the space you have available. First of all, you need to determine how much space you have in your garden or backyard and how much of it you're willing to dedicate towards a greenhouse.

If you don't have a lot of space, you could see if you have some space against your house, and if you do, then a lean-to greenhouse could be a great option for you. If you have some space in your garden or backyard, then you could consider getting a freestanding greenhouse. A greenhouse is a long-term investment, and I know many people who have regretted not getting a larger greenhouse when they could.

Greenhouse kits usually come in different sizes in 2 feet (60 cm) increments. I would suggest getting a greenhouse that is at least 6 feet (1.8 m) wide so that you have enough room to move around. Consider how many garden beds you'd like to have in your greenhouse, and also don't forget to have some space for a potting table and shelves—this will allow you to roughly plan for the size of your greenhouse.

Budget

Budget is perhaps one of the easiest but most important considerations to determine right from the start. It will determine the type and size of your greenhouse as well as your choice of materials.

If you have a lower budget, then you would likely have to consider getting a smaller greenhouse or one made from less expensive materials. Keep in mind that some materials are more durable than others. For example, glass is more expensive to buy initially than polycarbonate or polyethylene panels, but it will last a lifetime and will require little upkeep. Polycarbonate or polythene coverings, on the other hand, are cheaper to buy initially but will degrade over time and will need to be replaced.

If you live in a cold climate, you'll want to make sure to look for a well-insulated greenhouse. A cheap greenhouse kit might save you money at first, but in the long run they rarely end up being worth it—they fall apart quickly and have little insulation. Keep in mind that any supplemental heating is going to cost you money in the form of electricity bill.

Climate

If you live in a cold climate, you will need a well-insulated greenhouse if you want to grow plants year-round. Also, make sure it can withstand the elements, such as snow loads and strong winds. Insulation of different types of coverings was covered in the previous section, so you can refer to that to choose the material that suits your climate best. Beyond the insulation value of the covering material, you can also insulate the foundation, walls, and roof of your greenhouse. An inexpensive yet effective method is to use bubble wrap for insulation. You can find UV-stabilized polyethylene bubble wrap made especially for this purpose in some garden centers. I would recommend choosing wrap with large bubbles, as it has better insulating properties and lets in more light.

On the contrary, if the weather tends to be hot, you'll need a greenhouse with good ventilation to keep the inside cool. Overheating is the most common cause of plant failure in greenhouses. Your greenhouse should retain warm air during the colder months, but it also needs to have good ventilation in order to release hot air during the warmer months. When choosing a greenhouse, make sure to give consideration to the airflow. Look for vents near the top of the structure and base vents for air intake.

Roof vents are the most useful and ideally should be on both sides of the ridge and equivalent to 15–20% of the floor area. Side vents are not as good and are no substitute for roof ventilation. And while louvred vents can help regulate the air flow, they are hard to draught-proof in the winter.

Most greenhouses have manual vents that you'll need to open and close yourself, but there are also automatic openers that open or close in response to greenhouse temperatures. They can be useful, but they are slow to respond and need supplementing with manual control, such as opening some windows and the door each morning. Motorized vents activated by sensitive heat sensors are more efficient, but they are quite expensive for home use. Some greenhouse designs also feature exhaust fans to prevent overheating, and while it can be a nice feature to have, it's not necessary in most cases.

Materials

Both the structure and covering of greenhouses are available in different materials. You can go back to the previous section to check the pros and cons of different materials. Structures are often made out of aluminum, steel, wood, or plastic. Greenhouse covering is usually made from tempered glass, fiberglass, polycarbonate, or polyethylene film. Your choice of material for the frame will affect available covering materials. For example, greenhouses with plastic frames often support plastic or polyethylene sides, while greenhouses with metal or wood frames usually support glass or polycarbonate panes.

Additional Features

Many greenhouse kits only come with the bare bones of the greenhouse—the framing and covering. Things like work tables, shelving units, and benches usually need to be purchased separately. If you live in a cold climate, you might have to purchase a heating unit if you want to grow plants year-round. If plants don't get enough light in the winter, you might also need to get some grow lights. These additional costs are important to factor in when choosing a greenhouse.

Greenhouse Building Permit

Depending on where you live, you might need to a building permit if you want to build a greenhouse. This section will cover how you can find out whether you need a permit and how to go about getting one in case you do.

Zoning and building permits vary greatly across the US. The best course of action would be contacting your local zoning and building departments and consulting with them prior to building a greenhouse.

Zoning permits regulate the location of a greenhouse on a property. Zoning permits specify where you can build a greenhouse on your property—for example, how close to the lot lines you are permitted to build.

Building permits are typically issued by a county building department. While many rural areas do not require any permits for accessory or agricultural buildings, most urban areas have some requirements. One of the most important things to consider is whether you want a freestanding or an attached greenhouse. Attached greenhouses usually require a building permit because they are considered an addition to a home and not an accessory building.

Attached greenhouses are typically treated similarly to the addition of a sunroom. Building codes can vary greatly from community to community and have some requirements as to the appearance of the greenhouse. These rules are usually in place to maintain a high level of aesthetics in the neighborhood. In case your greenhouse doesn't meet the local requirements, you can apply for a variance. In most cases, a variance is possible because people like the idea of organic gardening in a greenhouse and local officials usually try to accommodate them.

As for other countries, in Canada, you would have to contact your local building office in order to find out whether you need a permit to build a greenhouse. The requirements will vary depending on your location. Ontario, for example, allows structures up to 160 square feet (14.8 sq. m) without requiring a permit as of 2024. The city of Calgary in Alberta requires anything over 100 square feet (9.3 sq. m) within the city to have a permit. So, it's best to contact your local building office to find out the current requirements prior to constructing your greenhouse.

In the UK, you can contact your local planning authority to find out whether you need a planning permission to build a greenhouse. Generally, you wouldn't need a planning permission to build a greenhouse in most cases. You might need it if you want to build a greenhouse in front of a garden, if the greenhouse covers more than half of the area of land around the "original house" (the house as it was first built or as it stood on 1 July 1948 if it was built before that date), if your greenhouse exceeds a certain height, and in some other cases too.

In Australia, you can contact your local council to check if you need a building permit. As a rule of thumb, freestanding non-permanent structures up to a certain size (usually 10 sq. m) do not need a permit, but always check with your local council prior to building a greenhouse.

I still remember when I got my first greenhouse. I didn't want to spend too much money and wanted a season extender rather than a year-round greenhouse, so I got a hoop house with plastic hoops and twin-wall polyethylene film. It worked really well and allowed me to extend the growing season as well as grow more heat-loving plants, like tomatoes, eggplants, peppers, and cucumbers. I liked it so much that I decided to build a year-round greenhouse. I built an A-frame greenhouse myself out of wood and recycled glass, and it worked quite well, but the frame started rotting after a few years. So, I decided to invest in a good-quality greenhouse kit and got a gable-style greenhouse with an aluminum frame and tempered glass glazing, which I still have to this day. It was one of the best purchases I've made in my life, and it's definitely worth every penny. Now I have a variety of greenhouses around my garden, including cold frames, hoop houses, a couple of gable-style greenhouses, and an abutting greenhouse at the back entrance of my house. I absolutely adore the fact that they allow me to grow fresh, delicious produce year-round, and I think they all have been some of the best investments I've made on my homestead.

Key takeaways from this chapter:

1. Greenhouses allow you to grow plants inside them year-round in most climates.
2. Greenhouses can be either attached or freestanding.
3. There are different styles of greenhouses, each with their pros and cons. Attached greenhouses include lean-to and abutting styles. Freestanding greenhouses include gable-style, A-frame, gothic arch, hoop house (Quonset), and geodesic dome shapes.
4. Greenhouse frames and coverings can be made out of different materials. Frames are typically made out of aluminum, stainless steel, wood or plastic. Covering is usually made out of tempered glass, fiberglass, polycarbonate, or polyethylene film and can be either transparent or diffused (opaque).
5. To choose the perfect greenhouse for you, you should consider your gardening needs, the space you have available, your budget, and the climate you live in.
6. You may need a permit in order to build a greenhouse. It's always best to contact your local authorities, such as zoning or building departments, in order to find out whether you need a permit prior to constructing your greenhouse.

The next chapter will cover planning your greenhouse, including choosing the perfect location for it and planning out the interior space. It will also cover the actual construction process. Finally, you will learn about gardening tools that might come in handy in order to make your gardening journey easier and more enjoyable.

Chapter 2: Planning and Building Your Greenhouse

A well-planned and well-built greenhouse will give you lots of gardening enjoyment as well as fresh, delicious produce year-round. Having a greenhouse will not only allow you to grow organic vegetables, fruits, and herbs year-round but also start your seedlings early and overwinter your delicate or tropical plants that can't stand the cold. Properly planning your greenhouse is key to successful year-round gardening.

With so many different options available, you might be wondering where the best location for your new greenhouse is, whether you want it attached to your home or freestanding in your garden, what type of materials you should use for framing, covering, and floors, and whether you'll need a permit to build it in the first place. These are all great questions, and all of them and many more will be answered in this chapter so that you can plan and build the perfect greenhouse for your needs.

Planning Your Greenhouse

As with any major purchase, a few key decisions must be made when buying a greenhouse. This section will cover all the important considerations you have to make when planning your greenhouse.

Attached or Freestanding

The first thing you should consider is whether you want your new greenhouse attached to your home or freestanding in your garden. Attached greenhouses typically have more convenient access, as you won't have to go outside, plus they are more energy efficient because one wall is already heated by your home. However, they do require a frost-free footer and foundation, which can add significant costs to the project.

Freestanding greenhouses typically have more flexibility in size and shape, and they also benefit from having more light coming in from all four sides, plus their foundations are typically lower in cost. In addition, building permits are usually less strict for freestanding greenhouses since they are considered a "temporary structure" or "accessory building", which brings us to the next important consideration.

Building/Zoning Permit

Once you've decided what type of greenhouse you want, you should contact your local authorities, such as zoning and building departments, and consult with them whether you need a building and/or zoning permit.

Location

Once you've got your permits sorted out, it's time to choose the perfect location for your greenhouse. One of the most common misconceptions about greenhouses is that they need to be located where they will get full sun exposure. While most plants need full sun exposure, what full sun actually means is that plants need 6–8 hours of direct sunlight per day. Placing your greenhouse facing south will give you full sun exposure, but you might need shade cloth to keep the greenhouse cool in the summer. West exposure will give you most afternoon sun, which is best for most plants, and east exposure will give you more morning sun, which is fine for most plants too. Only northern exposure in not ideal because it's too shady for most vegetable crops.

Sun Exposure

Speaking of plants' sun requirements, if you look at a seed packet or a plant label, you'll find the following terms that describe them:

- Full sun
- Full sun to partial shade
- Partial shade (or part shade)
- Dappled sun/shade
- Full shade

Full sun means that an area must receive 6–8 hours of direct sunlight on most days mostly between the hours of 10 a.m. and 4 p.m. Many plants need full sun to grow, flower, and produce fruit, but some plants can't handle the intense heat and/or dry conditions that often come with that much exposure to the sun. Mulching can help keep the soil cool and keep in moisture, and you can also add shade cloths to prevent your plants from getting burned by the sun (this will be discussed in more detail later in the book). When you choose plants, do some research on the species to determine if there are limitations on their full sun requirement. Plants that are sensitive to heat will usually come with a caution that they require some shelter from direct sunlight in mid-afternoon in hot climates.

The terms "partial (or part) sun" and "partial (or part) shade" are essentially the same and are often used interchangeably. Partial sun or partial shade means that an area must get 4–6 hours of sun exposure per day, preferably in the cooler hours of the morning. There is a subtle difference between these two terms, though. Partial sun puts greater emphasis on plants receiving at least the minimum sun requirements of 4–6 hours. These plants are typically more resistant to heat and need sunlight to flower and produce fruit, just not as much as plants that need full sun. Partial shade means that plants don't tolerate heat as well as plants that need partial sun, and they may need some relief from heat, especially in the afternoon. You can get shade cloths to provide some shade for these plants.

Dappled sun is a rare term, but you might find it used to describe sun requirements of a few plants. Dappled sun is similar to partial shade, but it means the sunlight filters through the branches and foliage of deciduous trees. Deciduous trees shed their leaves annually. Of course, you wouldn't build a greenhouse near a tree, but you can also get shade cloths to provide some shade for plants that need it. Woodland plants, such as trillium, Solomon's seal, and understory trees and shrubs, prefer dappled sun.

Full shade means that plants need 4 hours of sunlight mostly in the morning or late afternoon or a full day of dappled sunlight. Some people think that full shade means no sunlight at all, but that's not true. Very few plants, other than mushrooms, can survive without sunlight.

Once you have considered the space you have, you then need to spend some time monitoring which areas of the space receive sun and make notes of how this changes throughout the course of a day. The best way to measure average sunlight exposure is to simply observe the area where you plan to build your greenhouse every hour during the daylight hours over a week or two. Make notes to determine the average amount of sunlight the area receives each hour and where the shadows fall. Make notes whether it's full sun, filtered or dappled light, or full shade.

The path of the sun changes throughout the year, so it's best to measure the light in your garden during the growing season for your plants. You can make a note of how this changes over the seasons so that you're able to select the best plants for your garden.

You can also use flags or stakes to show the light and shadow in your yard. Or you could use some sheets of tracing paper and sketch the yard outline onto each page, then mark where the light and shade is every hour each time using a different sheet of tracing paper, and then you can layer the pages together to get an indication of how much light your yard receives.

If you don't personally have the time to monitor your garden each hour of the day, other options include purchasing a garden light meter, which may also measure soil moisture and pH levels too. Or you could take a picture of your garden every hour or set up a time-lapse camera that will do it for you. When you have a sun map, it's much easier to choose suitable plants for your garden by reading seed packets and seeing whether they like full sun, partial sun or shade, or full shade.

When you have determined the average amount of sunlight an area receives, you can choose plants that match the conditions your space has. If you don't have an environment that gets 6–8 hours of sunlight per day, then growing some vegetables may be tough, but you could still grow leafy greens, such as kale, spinach, Swiss chard, mustard greens, and lettuce, and also herbs, such as basil, parsley, mint, rosemary, oregano, thyme, sage, and chives. These leafy greens will give you so many good nutrients and vitamins, and herbs will really give your food a kick of flavor.

Accessibility and Utility Connections

Consider the accessibility of your greenhouse site for maintenance, watering, and electricity connections. As mentioned previously, attached greenhouses built at the entrance to your home are perhaps the easiest to access, as you don't even need to go outside, but if you want a freestanding greenhouse, make sure to build it in a convenient spot where you can access it relatively easily.

Ensure there's a clear pathway leading to the greenhouse entrance and sufficient space to maneuver equipment, such as wheelbarrows. If you plan to install utilities, such as electricity or water, consult with professionals to make the necessary connections safely.

Watering

Consider how easy it is to get water to where you plan to have your greenhouse. Ideally, you want your greenhouse to be near a water source because you'll need to water your plants weekly. If the weather is hot, you'll need to water your plants more often, and if you have a long way to fetch water, this makes it a more difficult task.

It's sensible to give some thought to water conservation. Consider if you could set up some water butts. Also, give thought to how to water your garden if you're ever away from home. Will a friend or a family member do this for you? You could also consider reservoirs with drip irrigation.

Most gardeners use watering cans to water plants in greenhouses. Most greenhouses aren't too big, so using a watering can is cheap and relatively easy. Having a water butt makes it easier to fill your watering cans, plus you might not have to carry them as far, depending on where your water source is. Having an outside tap makes it easier to water plants, as you can simply drag a hose to your greenhouse and water your plants. If your property has a well, you could hook a hose directly to the well for watering.

You can also opt for a drip irrigation system. Drip irrigation is a method for watering your garden that uses a system of pipes and valves connected to a water source, and it drips water onto the soil slowly. There are different types of drip irrigation systems, and this will be covered in more detail in Chapter 6.

Soil Quality

Soil is the very foundation of your garden, and it's important to always seek to improve and enrich it. Vegetables tend to like well-drained soil, which means that soil allows water to drain at a moderate rate and without water pooling and puddling.

If you have a lawn on your property, this can give you an indication of the health of your soil. If your lawn is lush and healthy, you probably have good soil. If your lawn is poor, your soil quality may need some work.

Even if your soil quality isn't great, don't worry—it's possible to improve it by adding organic matter. However, if the soil quality is really poor in your area, you could consider building raised beds, which work perfectly for greenhouses. Raised beds are typically filled with topsoil, compost, and things like coconut coir and peat moss. Building and filling raised beds will be covered in detail in Chapter 4.

Analyze the Environment

There may be things in your garden or backyard that can cause different conditions, so carefully analyze structures, trees and shrubs, and hard surfaces when you're considering a location for your garden.

You could have parts of your or your neighbor's property that casts shade. I have a part of my garden that is in the shade until later in the day just because of where the fence is. You should look at trees and hedges too. Some structures, like hedges, fences, and trees, may help protect your greenhouse from strong winds, but they may also create shade or could become snow drift areas in the winter. If you have hard surfaces, like rooftops, you could get water runoff from these, so do think carefully about where this water is running off onto so that you don't drown your greenhouse.

Vegetables planted in the shade aren't as productive as those in full sun and may be more susceptible to diseases and pest damage. If you live somewhere exceptionally hot, then plants may need some shade in the summer. You can use a shade cloth or plant taller plants nearby to create some shade.

If you have a larger greenhouse, you can also consider which side of your greenhouse faces north and which side faces south with regards to planting too. You can plant smaller crops in the south and taller plants in the north. For example, you can plant cabbage in the south and sugar snap peas in the north. This way, sugar snap peas won't cast too much shade on your cabbage.

Size

I would suggest that you spend some time thinking about how you plan to use your greenhouse. Consider how much growing space you need. Garden beds are typically 4 feet (1.2 m) wide so that you can access them without having to step of the soil, but you can make them narrower, of course. You also need some space for paths between the beds—3 feet (90 cm) wide should be enough for you to move freely around the greenhouse. Also, consider how tall your plants will grow once they are mature.

Greenhouse kits usually come in different sizes in 2 feet (60 cm) increments, most common being 8, 10, and 12 feet (2.4, 3, and 3.6 m) wide. I would suggest getting a greenhouse that is at least 6 feet (1.8 m) wide so that you have enough room to move around. In my experience, a 10-feet (3 m) wide greenhouse offers the most efficient utilization of space. Consider how many garden beds you'd like to have in your greenhouse, and also don't forget to have some space for a potting table and shelves—this will allow you to roughly plan for the size of your greenhouse.

Foundation

A greenhouse that is attached to your home or garage will require a frost-free footer and foundation so that it doesn't move separately from the permanent structure due to contraction and expansion of materials because of temperature changes. This will require excavation and concrete work, which will add cost to the installation.

If you want to save soil floors, then most smaller freestanding greenhouses can be built on a wood frame or a concrete wall if it is in a well-drained location. Brick and stone knee wall options are also quite popular because they can be beautiful and are more energy efficient. For hydroponics and growing in containers, a concrete slab foundation will work beautifully, although it is a more expensive option. One thing to keep in mind is that foundations for glass covered greenhouses 12x16 feet (3.6x4.8 m) or larger should have cement footers that extend below the frost line.

Frame

Different framing materials as well their pros and cons were covered in the previous chapter, which will hopefully help you choose the best type of greenhouse design and frame material for your needs. Consider how much snow your area gets and whether you have strong winds often. If you do get a lot of snow and strong winds, then having a metal frame (aluminum or stainless steel) is definitely recommended. Wood frames can be fine too; however, plastic frames and hoop houses are probably not the best for such weather conditions. Make sure to get a decent kit with welded aluminum truss designs, as they are the strongest. There are many cheap aluminum greenhouse kits that are made from flimsy stamped aluminum, and they often don't have the strength and rigidity to hold up in all weather conditions.

Covering/Glazing

Again, different covering materials were covered in the previous chapter, so you can refer to that to help you choose a covering material for your greenhouse.

Ventilation

Proper ventilation is very important, as it will allow to create the perfect conditions for your plants and prevent them from overheating during hot summer days. Most greenhouses have roof-mounted ridge vents along with side inlet vents (louvers). Warm air rises and escapes through the top, while cool, fresh is drawn in through the sides. This is usually enough in most cases, but if you live in a hotter climate, you should consider installing a powered ventilation system with a motorized intake shutter and an exhaust fan. These systems can cool down your greenhouse much more efficiently than passive ventilation with just vents. You can also have circulation fans that move air around the greenhouse, which can help prevent fungal and bacterial plant diseases. Another type of greenhouse fan is horizontal airflow (HAF) fan. They mix warm air near the roof with the cooler air on the ground, which helps create a uniform growing environment.

Heating

If you plan to grow plants all year round, you'll want to have a heater to keep your greenhouse warm on those cold winter nights, especially if you live in a colder climate. Small electric heaters are typically used in greenhouses 10x20 feet (3x6 m) or smaller, while gas heaters are usually used in larger greenhouses. Electric heaters are typically 100% energy efficient, while propane or natural gas heaters are 80% efficient. Gas heaters require a fresh air intake and exhaust, so you will need to have a 3–4-inch (7.5–10 cm) hole in your greenhouse.

Grow Lights

Depending on the location of your greenhouse and the climate you live in, your plants should usually get enough sunlight. However, if your plants don't get enough light during the winter or periods of cloudy weather, you can use grow lights to provide your plants with more light. Artificial lighting provided by grow lights should imitate the direct and indirect lighting requirements for your plants. Different plants have different needs, but typically your plants would need 8–10 hours of artificial light per day if they are getting some sunlight, and up to 16 hours if they don't get any sunlight.

The most common types of grow lights are LED, fluorescent, metal halide (MH), and high-pressure sodium (HPS).

LED grow lights are one of the newest forms of artificial lighting for plants. They are one of the most energy-efficient types of lighting. Plants need different light spectrums at different growth stages, and some LED grow lights (full-spectrum or RGB LEDs) can provide different light spectrums, which makes them really versatile.

Fluorescent grow lights give off a blue hue, and they are great for starting seeds and the beginning stages of seedlings. They have a low heat output, which allows seeds to grow without getting burned or drying out. They also work well for growing salad greens and flowers.

Metal halide (MH) grow lights are solid all-around lights. They provide the blue/white light spectrum, and they imitate sunlight during the summer months. They are mainly used for plants that have just finished sprouting and are now entering the growing or vegging stage. They also work well for long-day plants that require more light.

High-pressure sodium (HPS) grow lights give off an orangey-red hue, imitating the warmer colors of fall, and they work best for flowering and fruiting stages of your plants. Typically, you would use MH lights when your vegetables and fruits are starting to grow, and you would switch to HPS lights when your plants start flowering (you can simply change the bulbs, so you won't have to purchase a whole new set of grow lights).

MH and HPS grow lights are a popular choice for many greenhouse gardeners. They are cheaper than

LEDs, but they are less energy-efficient, they generate a lot of heat, plus they lose their effectiveness over time and their lifespan is shorter, so they need to be replaced more often. Even though the initial expense is higher when buying LED grow lights, they can last for years, unlike MH or HPS grow lights, which may only last a few seasons. Generally, full-spectrum LED grow lights are your best bet because they are highly versatile, energy efficient, and produce balanced white light that is similar to sunlight plants get in nature.

Plants need darkness just as much as they need light, so it's important to get a timer for your grow lights. It should be heavy-duty and grounded, and timers can be either manual or digital.

A rule of thumb is to have 20–40 watts per square foot of grow space. This means a 1000-watt LED grow light can cover 25–50 square feet (2.3–4.6 sq. m). The efficiency of your lighting system is the key to increasing the wattage. LED grow lights are the most efficient lights, and a 500-watt LED light can provide equivalent ratings to a 1000-watt MH or HPS light.

Additional Features and Accessories

Apart from having just garden or raised beds, you could think about having some extra features and accessories, like a drip irrigation system, a work bench or a potting table, some shelves, and so on.

While watering your plants can be a relaxing experience, it can take quite a bit of time and effort, especially if you have a bigger garden. You can make watering less of a chore by installing a drip irrigation system. Drip irrigation is the most effective way of watering your plants in my opinion. You can buy drip irrigation kits from garden centers or home improvement/hardware stores. Many kits are modular in design, which allows you to change your drip irrigation system as your garden changes. I would suggest making a plan of your greenhouse and taking it to a store so that they can suggest a kit that would fit your needs best. Drip irrigation kits are relatively affordable and are not very difficult to install and could be a nice addition to your greenhouse.

Having a work bench or a potting table in your greenhouse is very convenient if the space allows. It'll make starting seeds and potting up seedlings much more convenient. Having some shelves will allow you to store gardening tools and supplies and have everything you need at hand.

Building Your Greenhouse

So, once you've given a thorough thought to planning your greenhouse, now comes the exciting part of actually building it. Obviously, the process of building a greenhouse from a kit and from the ground up is a bit different, and both will be covered in this section.

First of all, remember to be safe. Having someone help you assemble your greenhouse is a tremendous help. Many steps will require assistance lifting and holding parts steady. Not all greenhouses need a foundation, but you may want one if your ground is not stable. If you're going to build your greenhouse on a foundation, you'll need to think how you will attach the frame to it. Use a tape measure and make the foundation slightly larger than the base of the greenhouse will be when it's finished. If you don't have the ability to lay a foundation, a portable greenhouse can be a good choice for you.

If you get a greenhouse kit, it should come with instructions to assemble it. If you decide to build your own greenhouse, you can find lots of different greenhouse plans online that you can further modify to suit your needs. You can also find some links to websites with great greenhouse plans at the end of the book in the resources section. With that said, let's take a look at the process of building your greenhouse step by step, from preparing the greenhouse site to actually building the greenhouse.

Greenhouse Site Preparation

Proper site preparation is very important, as it ensures you have a level foundation, adequate drainage, and optimal growing conditions for your plants.

Clearing the Area

First of all, you should clear the designated area of any vegetation or debris that may hinder the construction process. Remove things like rocks, tree stumps, and any other objects that could affect the stability or layout of your greenhouse. This will provide a clean and open space for your greenhouse structure.

Leveling the Ground

It's important to get this step right since you can't really correct it later on. You can use a shovel or a garden rake to remove any high spots and fill in any low areas. Once the soil is level, use a tamper, roller, or vibrating plate to flatten, even, and compact the soil. All these tools can usually be cheaply rented from a local tool shop. Ensure the entire area is even and smooth to prevent water pooling and uneven settling of the structure.

Addressing Drainage

Ensure the site is properly graded to allow water to flow away from the greenhouse. If necessary, you can dig a gentle slope around the greenhouse outline or install drainage pipes to divert excess water. The foundation needs to be flat, but having ground sloping around it helps water flow freely and prevents your soil from getting waterlogged.

Building the Foundation

The foundation will be the backbone that provides stability, support, and proper drainage for your greenhouse. If you have a smaller temporary greenhouse or a hoop house, then you'll likely won't need a foundation; however, even smaller greenhouses can benefit from a proper foundation, which will help keep the structure safe from the elements and protect the plants inside.

Greenhouse foundations are typically made out of wood or concrete. There are two types of concrete foundations: either a concrete slab (which is great for hydroponics and growing in containers) or a concrete wall (which will allow you to have a soil floor).

Wooden Foundation

Building a foundation out of wood works great for most home or backyard greenhouses. I would suggest using naturally resistant woods, such as cedar, cypress, or redwood. Pressure-treated wood also works well, but it contains copper, which is corrosive to aluminum. If you're going to have an aluminum frame, then you would need a 10-mil (0.25 mm) thick barrier between the wood and aluminum frame. Common barrier materials include polyethylene, vinyl, and plastic composite lumber.

First of all, you need to measure your greenhouse in order to determine the dimensions of your foundation. Use measuring tape and marking tools to determine the exact dimensions and layout of your greenhouse. Mark the perimeter of the foundation using stakes and string or chalk lines, ensuring precise placement according to your plans. As for material choice, I would recommend using 4x6-inch (10x15 cm) timbers for your foundation. You can cut the wood to size with a standard hand or power saw, or you could ask the guys at the lumber yard to cut it for you.

Once you have cut the wood to fit your greenhouse, you'll need to ensure the foundation is level. Lay the boards on the ground like you are going to set the greenhouse on them. Set a level on top of one of the boards. The horizontal bubble should be in-between the two lines marked on the level. This should be done for each board to ensure that the greenhouse base is level.

After ensuring the foundation has been leveled, it's now time to secure the boards together with lag screws. The lag screw should be 3 or more inches (7.5 cm) longer than the first board it is screwed through to insure a proper hold.

If you want to have soil floors, you can skip this step. However, if you'd like to grow in containers or hydroponically, then you'll need some type of ground cover to prevent weeds and grass from growing inside of your greenhouse. You can lay some landscaping fabric under the base and cut any excess fabric around the edges. Landscaping fabric will allow water to drain through the fabric while keeping weeds from growing in your greenhouse.

Now that the foundation has been built, it's important to make sure your base is square. To do so, use your tape measure, and take two diagonal measurements of the base—one from the front left corner to the back right corner and the other from the front right corner to the back left corner. You'll need to adjust the base until the two measurements are the same.

Now it's time to anchor the foundation to the ground. I would recommend using the earth anchor system because it's affordable, sturdy, and easy to install. Each earth anchor system includes 4 anchors (one for each corner of your base), 1 drive steel (used to drive anchors into the ground), and galvanized mounting hardware needed to secure the anchors to the base.

Step 1: First, place the earth anchor in the ground approximately 6 inches (15 cm) away from the corner of your greenhouse base. Put the drive steel inside of the anchor, and drive it into the ground using a hammer. A 3 or 4 lb (1.5–2 kg) hammer will be heavy enough to drive the anchor in most soils. You might need a larger hammer if you have hard soil, however. Drive the anchor until the end of the cable barely touches the edge of the greenhouse base.

Step 2: Once you have driven the anchor into the ground, pull the drive steel out of the ground, and insert it into the loop at the end of the cable. Pull cable out of the soil 2 to 3 inches (5–7.5 cm)—this will rotate the anchor into a locked (horizontal) position. Now you can mount the anchor to your greenhouse base.

Step 3: Take the loop at the end of your cable and place your lag bolt through it so that the cable is between your washers and the greenhouse base. Secure the lag bolt to the base and you are done. Do this for each corner of the greenhouse.

Concrete Wall Foundation

If you want to build a concrete wall foundation, it will have to be set on a footing below the frost line.

This type of foundation provides good support for heavier structures, like greenhouses glazed with glass. To build a wall, first you need to dig a trench in the soil to below the frost line and place forms for the footing. You can check with the local building inspector to determine what this depth is and to see if an inspection is required before the footing is poured. The footing is usually twice as wide as the wall and equally as thick.

After the footing has hardened, place the wall forms on top to pour the walls. The wall height should be a minimum of 6 inches (15 cm) above grade. At this point, you should install drains around the perimeter to drain water away from the greenhouse. The outside wall can be finished in several ways: you can leave it plain, paint it, or face it with brick or stone. You can attach an inch or two (2.5–5 cm) of insulation board to the inside or outside surface to help reduce heat loss.

Now you can backfill soil against the foundation and grade. Whether you build a concrete wall or a concrete slab foundation, you can, and I would highly recommend that you do that, fasten a 2x4-inch (5x10 cm) sill on the top of the foundation. It will act as an insulated buffer between the concrete and the greenhouse frame, which will help reduce heat loss. As for the choice of material, you can use woods, such as cedar, cypress, or redwood, or plastic composite lumber.

Concrete Slab Foundation

A concrete slab makes a convenient base for a greenhouse if you want to grow plants hydroponically or in containers. For an attached greenhouse, the finish floor is usually placed level with or one or two steps below the house floor. For a freestanding greenhouse, the floor should be several inches above the finish outside grade. I would recommend making the foundation an inch (2.5 cm) longer and wider than the greenhouse outside dimensions. A 3-inch-thick (7.5 cm) floor is sufficient for most greenhouses. The outside edges should be thicker to give support and resist cracking from frost. You would also need to put a drain in the center of the greenhouse slab that drains into a gravel pit or into a pipe leading to a drainage area outside the perimeter of the greenhouse. You would need at least 4 inches (10 cm) of compacted gravel or stone on top of the subsoil to provide drainage. Also, placing a 6-mil (0.15 mm) polyethylene moisture barrier on top of the gravel or stone will help keep the foundation dry.

To build the foundation, first build a form out of lumber around the perimeter. The top of the form should be at the finish floor height. You can add reinforcing wire or fiber to increase the strength of the slab. Once the concrete has set (usually about 24 hours), the forms can be removed. Insulation board 1 to 1.5 inches (2.5–3.8 cm) thick can be installed vertically around the outside of the foundation to a depth of 1 to 2 feet (30–60 cm). This will help insulate the floor and keep it warmer in the winter. As mentioned previously, you can also fasten a 2x4-inch (5x10 cm) sill on the top of the foundation, which will help provide additional insulation.

Building the Frame

If you've bought a kit, then it should come with assembly instructions. If you want to build your own greenhouse, follow the plan that you've decided to go with. Get all the necessary materials, and measure and cut frame parts—ensure accurate dimensions and smooth edges for proper assembly.

Then you can begin assembling the frame, starting at the base. Once the base is assembled, install the vertical uprights, and connect them to the base. These uprights will support the walls and provide structural rigidity for your greenhouse. If you've got a hoop house, then you would typically have to drive the ground posts into the ground using a ground post driver (these usually come in kits) and then put the hoops in.

After that, you can assemble the roof, attaching roof beams or rafters to the vertical uprights. If your greenhouse is small, you can assemble the roof separately and then put it onto the existing structure. If it's large or heavy, you'll probably need someone to help you with the assembly.

I would highly recommend adding support beams and crossbars to reinforce the greenhouse frame and enhance its strength. You can install support beams along the length and width of the greenhouse, connecting the vertical uprights. These beams will help distribute the weight of the roof and improve structural rigidity. You can also install crossbars horizontally across the frame, connecting the vertical uprights. These crossbars will provide additional strength and stability to the greenhouse structure.

You can attach the frame to the foundation using concrete anchor bolts, which are available at most hardware stores. Set bolts within a foot (30 cm) of each corner, then space additional anchor bolts about 4 feet (1.2 m) apart.

Greenhouse Covering/Glazing

Once the frame is up, you can move on to installing the covering. First of all, ensure that the greenhouse frame is clean, free from debris, and structurally sound. Fix any weak or damaged areas before proceeding with installing the covering.

To install the covering, begin by attaching the covering material at one end of the greenhouse frame. Secure it using clips, screws, or other fasteners suitable for your chosen material. Avoid anything that could damage or make holes in the covering. If you have a hoop house, then you would have to cover it with polyethylene film and secure it at the ends of the framework, usually using double spline extrusions and special latches.

Sealing and weatherproofing your greenhouse covering is important to prevent heat from escaping and water from getting in. Use weatherstripping or specialized greenhouse tape to seal gaps between the covering and the frame, especially at the edges, seams, and joints. Caulk also works great as an insulating layer. It's cheap, easy to use, and works to keep dirt, water, and debris out of your greenhouse. If you choose a double or triple-walled covering material, like polycarbonate, ensure that the channels between the layers are clean and free from debris.

If your kit comes with vents, windows, or fans, make sure to properly install them. You can also add shade cloths or blinds to help regulate light intensity and reduce excessive heat buildup during hot weather. If you plan to install utilities, such as electricity or water, consult with professionals to make the necessary connections safely.

I still remember when I built my first greenhouse, which was actually a hoop house. I got a kit at a garden center and was so excited to go back to my homestead and start building it! I first cleared the greenhouse site and then moved on to driving the posts into the ground. I then unfolded the polyethylene film over the greenhouse and secured it at the ends of the framework. I grew a ton of cucumbers that year, and we made lots of pickles to preserve them. I still have that greenhouse, and although I've had to replace the covering, other than that, it's been great. Since then, I've got a few more greenhouses, but my first greenhouse still holds a special place in my heart!

Key takeaways from this chapter:

1. Planning your greenhouse properly is essential to its success. You'll have to consider what type of greenhouse you want, which will also determine whether you need a zoning and/or planning permit. Then you'll need to choose a location that gets plenty of sun and is easily accessible. You will also have to choose what type of materials you want to use for your greenhouse. Ventilation is very important, and you'll need to make sure your greenhouse has at least some vents, but you could also go for an exhaust fan along with intake louvres, which is more effective. Depending on your climate, you might need to consider whether your greenhouse will need heating and/or grow lights. Finally, you can consider having some additional features and accessories, like a drip irrigation system, a work bench or a potting table as well as some shelves.

2. Placing your greenhouse facing south will give you full sun exposure, but you might need shade cloths to keep the greenhouse cool in the summer. West exposure will give you most afternoon sun, which is best for most plants, and east exposure will give you more morning sun, which is fine for most plants too. Only northern exposure in not ideal because it's too shady for most vegetable crops.

3. Before starting to build your greenhouse, you will need to prepare the greenhouse site first by clearing the area from things like rocks and debris and leveling the ground. Then you can move on to building a foundation if your greenhouse needs one. After that, you'll need to assemble the frame and anchor it to the ground. Next, you'll need to install the covering. And finally, if you plan to install utilities, such as electricity or water, consult with professionals to make the necessary connections safely.

The next chapter will move on to explaining how you can actually use your greenhouse to create the perfect growing environment for your plants, looking at regulating temperature, humidity, and light. It will also cover which plants are best to grow during different seasons.

Chapter 3: Greenhouse Environment

So, you've finally got your own greenhouse! You must be excited to start growing lots of different lovely plants in it; however, there are a few things you need to know to create the perfect growing environment for your plants. One of the best things about greenhouses is that they allow you to control the environment inside them, including temperature, humidity, and light, which allows you to tailor the growing conditions to your plants' needs. You do need to know what you're doing, though, and keep the environment inside your greenhouse bearable during the summer and warm enough during the colder months because otherwise your plants can get too hot or too cold. So, this chapter will cover everything you need to know to create the best possible growing environment for your plants so that you can get the most out of your greenhouse.

Temperature

While greenhouses allow you to keep your plants relatively warm during the winter months, they can get too hot in the summer. Different plants prefer different growing conditions, and you can find the ideal temperature for specific plants in plant profiles in Chapter 9. In general, in the summer, the ideal greenhouse temperature is 75–85°F (24–30°C) during the daytime and 60–75°F (15–24°C) at night. In the winter, greenhouse temperature should be around 65–70°F (18–21°C) during the day and 45°F (7°C) at night. These temperature ranges are generally suitable for most plants.

Useful Tools

Before moving on to adjusting the temperature inside your greenhouse, let's first take a look at a few tools that will come in useful. Two essential tools you should have are a thermometer and a hygrometer. They will allow you to monitor two critical variables in plant development—temperature and humidity. You can get digital 2-in-1 thermometer/hygrometer devices, which I would recommend, as they give more accurate readings. They can also measure minimum/maximum temperature and humidity levels over a period of 24 hours, which is helpful. There are also smart models that allow you to keep track of statistics and monitor the temperature constantly via a mobile app.

You can also get a greenhouse temperature alarm system, and it can identify issues such as temperature fluctuations and notify you via phone, email, or text in case of extreme changes, which is really helpful.

Finally, automatic vent openers can be quite convenient. They open the vents in your greenhouse automatically and allow hot air to escape while letting fresh air in. They usually don't even need electricity and work depending on the temperature. Once heat builds up within the cylinder mechanism of the opener, the vent begins to open, and after the air inside your greenhouse cools down, the vent closes. It is a rather popular tool among greenhouses gardeners, as you won't have to check on your plants all day long, plus it can work when you are away and keep your plants safe.

Now that you know how to monitor the temperature in your greenhouse and the tools that can help you, let's take a look at how you can actually adjust the temperature inside your greenhouse.

Controlling Greenhouse Temperature

There are a variety of tools at your disposal when it comes to adjusting greenhouse temperature. First, let's take a look at ventilating and cooling your greenhouse during the hot summer months, and then we'll move on to heating your greenhouse during the winter.

Regulating Heat

In the summer, your greenhouse can get quite hot, so it's important to monitor the temperature inside it and ventilate your greenhouse to help cool it down when needed. There are a variety of ways to cool down your greenhouse, including using vents, fans, air conditioners, shade cloths, misting systems, and more, all of which will be covered below.

Ventilating Your Greenhouse

One of the easiest things you can do to help cool down your greenhouse during the hot summer months is simply to open the doors and vents or windows of your greenhouse to facilitate natural ventilation. Make sure to open both wall and roof vents—since hot air rises, it will escape from the vents above, and cool, fresh air will enter from the wall vents. If you have a hoop house with polyethylene covering, you can roll it up to vent the warm air out. Some greenhouses have hinged roofs that can be opened to provide air circulation. If your greenhouse has fans—that's great! You can turn them to help with ventilation when the temperature inside your greenhouse gets a bit too hot.

Shade Cloths

Shading is an efficient and cost-effective method that can help regulate the temperature inside your greenhouse. Shade cloths are curtains that roll out over rails placed above your crops. You can put them up to prevent the sun from scorching your plants. When choosing a shade cloth, consider its transmission level. In general, 30–50% works great for most vegetables. I personally prefer using 40% shade cloths.

Air Conditioner

If you live in a climate with really hot and humid summers, you may consider installing an air conditioner unit. Not only do they help cool down your greenhouse, but they also have a dehumidifying feature that helps alleviate high humidity issues.

For a greenhouse, you would typically get compact units, such as mini-split, window AC, or portable systems. They provide a simple but efficient way to cool your greenhouse. You can also combine them with smart controllers, which will help automate your greenhouse environment. They can be a bit costly, plus they'll need some maintenance, but they are the most effective way to cool down your greenhouse.

Misting/Fogging System

A misting or fogging system produces fine mist at regular intervals to help control greenhouse temperature, and it also helps increase humidity, which can be beneficial for vegetative plants as well as baby and micro plants. The main drawback of such systems is that water on the leaves of your plants and increased humidity can lead to fungal diseases, so you'll need to inspect your plants periodically. Personally, I'm not a huge fan of these systems. But if you live in a dry climate, they are really convenient and effective at increasing humidity.

Damping Down

Damping down means simply putting water on hard surfaces, such as staging and paths. When cold water evaporates, it provides a cooling effect in the greenhouse. You can do it once in the morning and once in the evening.

Wet Wall

A wet wall is a cooling device that uses a pump to circulate water through the wall and a fan on the opposite side of the wet wall to cool down the evaporated water. The water is recirculated and continuously cools the air in the grow environment. When using a wet wall, it is important to monitor humidity levels and cut off the water supply to the wet wall if the humidity is getting too high.

Heating Your Greenhouse

In the winter during the daytime, a greenhouse can usually generate enough heat to keep your plants warm. However, during the night, temperatures can drop drastically, which means you would likely need a heating solution. Depending on your weather conditions, you can utilize the heat generated throughout the day or install a heating system.

Insulating Your Greenhouse

If you live in a mild climate, then simply insulating your greenhouse to help keep the heat in may be enough to get you through the winter. You can seal the roof and walls with silicone caulk to avoid heat loss through small cracks and gaps. As mentioned previously, bubble wrap is a great insulating material. You can layer the sides and roof of your greenhouse with it, and it will radiate heat in your greenhouse for hours even after sunset. You can also consider insulating the north wall with plywood or other thick material—this will help trap the heat, as this side gets minimal sunlight, plus it will help the frigid north winds from seeping in.

Adding Thermal Mass

Thermal mass are materials that can absorb heat and release it when needed, and it is perhaps one of the easiest ways to heat your greenhouse. For instance, water has a high thermal mass, so you can use it to heat your greenhouse.

To create thermal mass, you can fill large barrels or containers with water and place them somewhere where the sun shines for most of the day. Then put a loose lid on, and leave them in your greenhouse. The sun will heat the water during the day, and it will release the heat gradually to the greenhouse at night. If you decide to use this method, make sure to change the water every week to avoid bacteria, algae, or fungus growth.

Electric Space Heaters

Electric space heaters work great for heating small spaces by circulating hot air. They are convenient and portable and are ideal for small greenhouses. Many gardeners use them because they are a safe and clean option as opposed to fuel-based heaters. They do not release any dangerous chemicals; however, they can be a safety hazard. Make sure the one you choose comes with a safety switch to avoid that.

Ductless Heat Pumps

Ductless heat pumps are essentially like AC, but they heat the air instead of cooling it down. These devices are more costly than electric space heaters, but they can be very powerful and can heat even bigger greenhouses with ease. There are different types of ductless heat pumps, including mini-splits, window heat pumps, and portable ones.

Ductless mini-splits are perhaps the most common type of heat pumps and provide both cooling and heating. They are energy efficient and are easy to install—you can do it yourself even if you have minimal DIY skills. They are the best option if you are looking for an all-in-one solution for your greenhouse.

Window heat pumps are also popular among many greenhouse gardeners. They are rather small and typically look like a box. When installing a window heat pump, make sure to seal all the gaps to avoid cold air from seeping in. You can also get through-the-wall variations of this device. They are similar to window units but are made to sit inside a wall opening instead of a window.

Portable heat pumps are somewhat similar to electric space heaters. They are small, compact, stand-alone units and can be taken anywhere easily. They do not require installation, but they have an exhaust pipe that needs to be vented outside through a window or a wall opening.

Just like AC units, ductless heat pumps can be made smart with smart AC controllers—this will allow you to monitor and control your unit using your phone, use scheduling to set different daytime and nighttime temperatures for your plants, and maintain the perfect climate in your greenhouse.

Hydronic Heating Systems

Hydronic heating systems use hot water pipes to heat your greenhouse. These systems are rather complicated and include a boiler, a hot water piping system, and a controller. The boiler heats the water, which is then distributed via a piping system installed underground. A controller with a temperature sensor monitor is used to keep track of the temperature settings. These systems are quite expensive and are typically used in commercial settings and/or really cold climates.

Humidity

Along with the temperature, it's important to control the humidity inside your greenhouse to prevent the spread of pests and diseases while keeping your plants happy and not drying them out at the same time. You can control humidity by making changes to your ventilation, heating, watering, and more.

High humidity can promote the growth of powdery mildew, botrytis blight, and other fungal diseases as well as reduce yields of your plants. On the contrary, low humidity can cause your plants to dry out and require a lot more water, which typically results in stunted growth.

Different plants may prefer different conditions, but in general, the ideal humidity level for most plants in a greenhouse is about 80% at 80°F (27°C). At this level, most greenhouse plants have the best yields and highest growth rates. Keep in mind that temperature affects humidity. Higher temperatures lead to more evaporation, which lowers humidity. The opposite is true for lower temperatures. As mentioned previously, you can monitor both temperature and humidity using a thermometer/hygrometer combo.

With that said, let's take a look at the ways to control the humidity inside your greenhouse.

Water Only When Necessary

Watering your plants increases humidity, so the cheapest and easiest way to reduce humidity in your greenhouse is to water your plants only when necessary. Watering your plants will be covered in detail in Chapter 5, but in short, I recommend watering your plants deeply usually once a week (or twice if the weather is really hot). This is best for most plants, plus it helps avoid raising the humidity too much.

On the contrary, if you need to increase humidity, you can simply mist or spray some water around the greenhouse. As the water evaporates, it'll add moisture to the air. This is even more effective at night when the greenhouse is heated up already.

You can also place trays or buckets of water around the greenhouse. The water will evaporate from these containers, and it will increase the humidity in the air. This works well in smaller greenhouses, but it may not be as effective in larger ones. Plus, standing water can also attract pests and other insects.

Ventilation

Ventilation not only helps control the temperature inside your greenhouse but also the humidity. Good ventilation is key to preventing fungal diseases. Ventilating your greenhouse helps stale, humid air escape, while letting fresh air in. You can increase or decrease ventilation by opening or closing vents or turning fans on or off if you have them. This method works well in the summer, but it's not great in the winter, as you will likely require excessive heating to compensate for the heat loss caused by ventilating.

Heating

If you have a heater, then heating your greenhouse can help control or reduce the humidity because higher temperatures cause more evaporation. This method will only work during the colder months, but it's a nice and easy way to regulate both temperature and humidity inside your greenhouse.

Using a Dehumidifier

Dehumidifiers can be quite costly, but they are very efficient. If you live in a very humid climate, they might be worth the investment. Dehumidifiers not only help reduce the moisture in the air but also improve the air circulation. Dehumidifiers don't draw air from the outside, which is great to keep the warm air inside in the winter.

There are two different types of dehumidifiers—chemical and mechanical. Chemical dehumidifiers use a hygroscopic solution saturated in salt that draws moisture from the air, while mechanical dehumidifiers use refrigerator techniques or heat pump systems.

On the contrary, if you want to increase humidity, you can use a humidifier. They essentially add water vapor to the air and are very effective at boosting humidity levels. There is a wide variety of humidifiers on the market, from small, portable units to larger ones designed for commercial growing spaces.

Light

So, you've learned how to control temperature and humidity in your greenhouse; however, many gardeners tend to forget that controlling light is essential too. Sunlight conditions in greenhouses can vary rapidly, affecting temperature, humidity, and the amount of light your plants get. In the summer, the scorching heat can burn your plants, and in the winter, your plants may not get enough light because of short light hours and cloudy weather. There are two ways you can control how much light your greenhouse plants receive, which are shading and grow lights. Let's take a closer look at both of them.

Shading

Shading was already mentioned in the section on controlling temperature, but it also helps save your plants from scorching heat in the summer. If your plants tend to wilt and dry out due to excessive heat, you can put up a shade cloth during the hottest hours of the day, usually around midday and in the afternoon. This will help prevent the sun from burning your plants as well as lower the temperature in the greenhouse.

Grow Lights

On the contrary, if your plants don't get enough light, for example, in the winter or if the weather is cloudy, you can get grow lights to provide them with additional light. Choosing grow lights for your greenhouse was covered in Chapter 1, so you can refer back to that section.

Artificial lighting provided by grow lights should imitate the direct and indirect lighting requirements for your plants. Different plants have different needs, but typically your plants would need 8–10 hours of artificial light per day if they are getting some sunlight, and up to 16 hours if they don't get any sunlight. Remember that plants need darkness just as much as they need light, so don't keep them on all day long. You can get a timer for your grow lights, which is very convenient.

Greenhouse Seasons

Depending on the climate you live in, the type of greenhouse you have, and whether you have supplemental heating, you may be able to grow plants year-round. Even if you live in a really cold climate, a greenhouse will extend your growing season considerably. Let's take a look at different greenhouse seasons and what plants are best suited for different times of the year.

Spring

Every gardener looks forward to the start of the spring season. You can start preparing for spring in late winter by harvesting your winter plants and clearing the garden beds. Spring is the perfect time to start seeds, so you could start some plants for transplanting. To germinate seeds, you'll need interior temperatures to be in the 65–75°F (18–24°C) range. In early spring, you could start some hardy plants, including peas, broccoli, Swiss chard, garlic, onions, shallots, cabbage, lettuce, leaks, Brussels sprouts, and much more. During the middle of spring, you can start fast-growing tender plants, including cucumbers, squashes, pumpkins, zucchini, melons, and beans. You can start these plants in your greenhouse and then transplant them to your garden after the last frost or keep them growing in the greenhouse.

Summer

The hot summer weather is perfect for growing heat loving plants, such as tomatoes, cucumbers, peppers, and melons. These plants do love heat; however, if temperatures climb really high in the day, above 90°F (32°C) for example, this can damage them. Remember to keep your greenhouse ventilated, and add shades if necessary. Also, watch the humidity levels, and spray some water around your greenhouse to keep it up if needed. In late summer, you can sow lettuce, salad leaves, and baby carrots for fall harvest. You could also plant new potatoes, which will be ready for Christmas time.

Fall

If you live in a climate where winter temperatures regularly dip below freezing and you don't want to have to heat your greenhouse too much in the winter, then you could plant cool-season plants that prefer lower temperatures, such as lettuce, onions, kale, collard greens, radishes, and some herbs.

With the winter approaching, you won't be able to transplant your crops outside, so consider the length of their growing season and the amount of space they will need before planting longer maturing plants, such as beets, carrots, leeks, and cabbage.

Winter

What you can grow in the winter will depend on your climate, the type of greenhouse you have, and whether you have some form of heating. You could potentially even grow tomatoes if it gets warm enough where you live or if you can afford to heat your greenhouse and keep grow lights on. However, this is obviously neither practical nor economically viable in most cases, so you would likely have to grow some cool-season crops that prefer lower temperatures, like leeks, radishes, turnips, beets, carrots, and potatoes. You can also grow flowers if you'd like—you can use them to decorate your home or sell them at a local farmers' market. Popular winter flowering plants include Amaryllis (grown from bulbs), orchids, gladioluses, pansies, lilies, and impatiens.

Key takeaways from this chapter:

1. You can control the environment inside your greenhouse, including temperature, humidity, and light, which allows you to tailor the growing conditions to your plants' needs.

2. Two essential tools you should have to monitor the temperature and humidity inside your greenhouse are a thermometer and a hygrometer. You can get digital 2-in-1 units, which I would personally recommend doing, because they are accurate and easy to use.

3. You can lower the temperature in your greenhouse by ventilation, using an AC unit, shade cloths, a misting system, a wet wall, or simply spraying some water around your greenhouse and on the surfaces, which is known as damping down.

4. To increase the temperature in your greenhouse, you can insulate it to help prevent heat loss, add some thermal mass, such a water barrel, which will help retain heat, or you could use a portable electric heater, a ductless heat pump, or a hydronic heating system.

5. Along with the temperature, it's important to control the humidity inside your greenhouse to prevent the spread of pests and diseases, while at the same time keeping your plants happy and not drying them out. You can control humidity by making changes to your ventilation, heating, watering, and more. Keep in mind that temperature affects humidity. Higher temperatures lead to more evaporation, which lowers humidity. The opposite is true for lower temperatures.

6. To lower humidity, water your plants only when necessary (usually a deep watering once or twice a week), ventilate it, raise the temperature, or use a dehumidifier.

7. To increase humidity, you could spray some water around your greenhouse and on the surfaces or use a humidifier.

8. Controlling light exposure of your plants is important too. There are two ways you can control how much light your greenhouse plants receive, which are shading and grow lights. In the summer, the scorching heat can burn your plants, so you can use shade cloths to help avoid that. And in the winter, your plants may not get enough light because of short light hours and cloudy weather, so you can use grow lights to provide them with additional light.

9. Depending on the climate you live in, the type of greenhouse you have, and whether you have supplemental heating, you may be able to grow plants year-round. Spring is the perfect time to start seeds and grow some hardy plants, like peas, broccoli, Swiss chard, garlic, onions, shallots, cabbage, lettuce, leaks, Brussels sprouts, and more. During the middle of spring, you can start fast-growing tender plants, including cucumbers, squashes, pumpkins, zucchini, melons, and beans. You can start these plants in your greenhouse and then transplant them to your garden after the last frost or keep them growing in the greenhouse. The hot summer weather is perfect for growing heat loving plants, such as tomatoes, cucumbers, peppers, and melons. In late summer, you can sow lettuce, salad leaves, and baby carrots for fall harvest. You could also plant new potatoes, which will be ready for Christmas time. In the fall, you could plant lettuce, onions, kale, collard greens, radishes, and some herbs. And in the winter, you can grow some cool-season crops that prefer lower temperatures, like leeks, radishes, turnips, beets, carrots, and potatoes.

The next chapter will look at preparing garden beds for planting as well as building raised beds in case you'd prefer to go this route. It will also cover the essential tools you will need as a gardener and will also suggest a few tools that might be handy to have.

Chapter 4: Soil—Creating the Perfect Growing Medium

The soil is one of the most important things in your garden. It is the medium that gives the nutrients and moisture to your vegetables, herbs, and flowers to help them grow and create delicious produce. A key mantra for organic gardeners is "feed the soil, not the plant", and organic gardening is all about replenishing the soil and leaving it in a better condition than before and taking good care of it so that it can take care of your plants and feed you and your family for generations to come. This chapter is moving on to the really practical hands-on part of preparing your garden beds for planting as well building raised beds if you'd prefer to go that route.

Gardening Tools

If you're getting into greenhouse gardening, it's highly likely you have some gardening experience already, and you probably have a garden and some gardening tools. With that said, there are so many tools you can buy in your local garden center that it's hard to figure out what you actually need in the garden. In this section, I'd like to cover the essential tools you will need as a gardener. I will also suggest a few tools that might be handy to have.

To explain why you need certain tools, we'll look at the whole process, from starting your garden to harvesting the delicious produce. This book is based on the no-dig method (which is perfect for greenhouse gardening), so we'll follow the process of building your garden according to this method. It will be covered in-depth later in this chapter, but in short, it involves covering the ground with cardboard to kill the weeds first, then layering compost, straw, and other organic materials, and finally, creating indentations for planting vegetables.

1. Gloves

Gardening is a lovely hobby, but it can quickly turn into a hassle without the right pair of gloves. Make sure to get gloves that are durable but not too bulky, especially for working with seeds or transplanting seedlings. Ensure they fit well too, as poorly fitting gloves can cause blisters or result in accidents from slipping off. The fabric should ideally be water resistant but also breathable—this will help keep your hands cool and comfortable. Longer cuffs will help protect your wrists and forearms from scratches and keep the soil from getting in.

2. Pitchfork

You'll need to move a lot of compost to build no-dig garden beds, and a pitchfork is perfect for that. It's also great for turning your compost pile and moving loose materials.

3. Rake

Rake is used to create a level working area once you've layered your garden beds. A good rake should have a sturdy handle, and the prongs should be made out of one piece of metal. Raking is all about spreading out topsoil to create a level surface and also loosening the topsoil to prepare garden beds for planting. This helps improve drainage and prevent water logging issues, and it also allows for better water absorption in the soil.

4. Trowel

So, your bed is leveled and ready for some transplants. For this, you can use a trowel. I'd suggest getting a high-quality trowel because cheaper ones may look good at first glance, but they break or bend easily and will probably not last you one season. This will be your tool for moving small amounts of soil, transplanting your vegetables, and weeding in tight spaces where it's hard to use a hoe.

5. Hoe

Garden hoes come in many different varieties: Dutch hoe, draw hoe, heart-shaped hoe, and more. The most common is the Dutch hoe, but we mainly use a straight hoe. Stirrup or shuffle hoes are great for shallow hoeing—it's a technique for weeding, and this will be covered in more detail in Chapter 6.

A hoe is a great tool for getting rid of weeds. To use your hoe for weeding, hold it as you would hold a broom, and angle it so the blade goes just below the surface. This way, you can slice off the tops from weeds.

6. Watering Can

As mentioned previously, there are a lot of ways to water your garden, and watering it using watering cans can be a daunting task. However, it can be fine if you have a smaller garden, and especially if you have a water butt so that you don't have to carry heavy watering cans from your house. Even though watering by hand can be quite a task, it's also a good moment to inspect your vegetables and your soil, picking out some weeds as you go.

7. Pruners/Scissors

Pruners come in really handy when it's time to harvest your crop. You don't need to get really expensive ones. Just make sure they have a comfortable grip and look like they won't fall apart after one use.

There are two main styles of pruners: bypass and anvil. In bypass pruners, blades bypass each other to make the cut. In anvil pruners, blade slams on top of a ridge. I personally prefer bypass pruners because they seem to cut cleaner, and it's important to make clean cuts with your pruners so that you don't hurt your plants. Pruners need to be kept sharp, so if a blade goes dull, sharpen or replace it because dull pruners can damage plants.

8. Spade/Shovel

Even though no-dig gardening is about trying to disturb the soil as little as possible, you might have to do some digging when dealing with bigger plants. For this, you can either get a spade or a shovel. I personally prefer a spade because it's made to really get in the soil and dig it up. Some spades have bend-over tops to rest your foot on, which makes them a bit more comfortable to use. With no-dig gardening, you won't have to use it much, so your spade will probably last you a lifetime.

9. Dibber

Dibbers are used to make holes when planting seeds or transplanting seedlings. You can use a trowel for transplanting seedlings, but a dibber can come in really handy. You simply need to put some weight on it, and you'll make a nice gap for your transplants—it's really easy to pop in your plants this way.

10. Hedge Shears

Hedge shears are meant to trim hedges, but they are a great tool for trimming or cutting down plants around the garden. After the harvest, for most plants it's time to go, so you can pull them out or cut them down with shears and add them to your compost pile. I usually cut the plants down because roots will decompose and feed the soil, so hedge shears come in really handy.

11. Wheelbarrow

Getting a wheelbarrow inside a greenhouse can be challenging sometimes, but you'll need to move compost and mulch around, so a wheelbarrow will definitely come in handy. You'll need it only sporadically, though, so that's something to think about. Think if you could borrow one for a few days—this will help you save some money and space. If you decide to get a wheelbarrow, make sure it stays inside when not using it. That's all you need to do to keep it for many years. If your shed is small, you can also "park" it with the handles turned up against the wall.

Preparing Garden Beds

You might think you'll have to dig and turn over your garden beds, which can be quite challenging to do inside a greenhouse with limited space, but what if I told you that you can get healthier, more fertile soil by leaving it alone? Digging is done to loosen and aerate the soil, and it's often considered a necessity when it comes to preparing garden beds for new plants. But not only can it lead to back and joint pain and even blisters when performed at length, it's also not that good for your soil.

Don't get me wrong, digging does have certain benefits, such as loosening up and aerating soil and helping organic matter, like crop residue and weeds, decompose faster. However, disturbing the soil by digging can damage the soil structure and lead to soil compaction, which means plants' roots will have a harder time permeating the compacted soil. It can also harm the microorganisms living in it, which play an important role in maintaining a healthy soil environment. Digging can lead to increased weed growth, as you can expose weed seeds when digging and turning over soil. So, in many cases, digging can actually do more harm than good.

Fortunately, there is a method that eliminates the need for digging all together, and it's called no-dig gardening (also known as no-till gardening). It is more than just a way to skip over the mundane chore of digging your soil, though. This technique, which involves layering cardboard, compost, and organic matter, like straw, protects important microorganisms in your soil, reduces the number of weeds you get, and minimizes soil erosion. Though it requires some work and patience at first, in the long run, no-dig gardening is easier, less time consuming, and more beneficial to your garden ecosystem. Plus, it works perfectly for greenhouses, as you won't have to dig or till your garden beds ever.

There is a variety of methods you can use to start no-dig garden beds, such as the no-dig gardening method, lasagna gardening, hugelkultur, and others. They do have a lot in common, though. Most no-dig gardening methods recommend just covering the area with cardboard and/or newspapers and building garden beds on top of it by layering organic materials, such as compost, hay, kitchen scraps, and more. This works really well even if you have not so great soil, plus it allows you to have great results rather quickly—you can usually start planting right after setting up your garden beds, and the cardboard or newspapers will decompose by the time the plants' roots reach it.

However, these methods do have their cost. You will need quite a bit of organic matter, including compost, straw, and kitchen scraps, plus you will have to bring them in to your garden beds. With that said, making your own compost is not difficult at all, and it will be covered in detail in Chapter 6. Not only will it help you build your soil, but it also uses things you usually throw away in the trash, so it's a win-win situation.

The no-dig method is about trying not to disturb the soil at all or keep the disturbance to a minimum and leaving things like organic matter on the surface of the soil. The organic matter feeds the soil (which is what happens in nature) and helps with drainage and aeration. In nature, leaves fall off trees onto the ground, and bacteria and fungi attack them and turn them into natural compost. Then creatures like earthworms and beetles carry the decomposed material deeper into the soil where plants' roots can use the nutrients.

The no-dig method is suited to all types of soil, even heavy clay. The soil stays healthy because it's not disturbed, and you get healthier, stronger plants. You don't use a fork or a spade to loosen or dig the soil, so you don't disturb the microorganisms, the fungi, and the worms in it. Your soil will retain more moisture, and you'll get fewer weeds. You will also end up using less fertilizers and pesticides. Plus, you won't get backache or blisters on your hands from needing to dig the soil.

With the no-dig gardening method, you simply enrich your soil by adding compost as well as nitrogen- and carbon-rich materials to it. These layers break down to create a fantastic growing environment for your plants. The no-dig method is an organic gardening approach that emulates nature, and it can be used in gardens of any size. The first year that you do no-dig may be the most demanding because you may need to prepare your garden beds, which includes removing rocks, grass, and weeds and adding compost and organic matter, but I promise it does get easier ever after and is definitely worth it in the long run.

How to Start a No-Dig Garden Bed

Charles Dowding was the person who first started the no-dig method, and he suggests initially starting out with a small area of 4 by 8 feet (1.2 by 2.4 m). He states that you can get just as good a harvest from this area as a larger area, and he uses a space like this to do succession planting all year long. In Dowding's vast experience, he has found that using the no-dig method results in much better harvests than when you cultivate your soil. You can start a no-dig bed by layering compostable materials like a lasagna.

Here's how you start a no-dig garden bed:

1. Prepare the Area and Cover It in Light-Blocking Material

To start a no-dig garden bed, you need to remove rocks and weeds first. You would have cleared your greenhouse site before building the greenhouse anyway, but if you still got some weeds or rocks, make sure to remove them. You can cut the weeds at the ground level and add them to your compost pile. Then use cardboard or newspapers to block out the sunlight so that weeds can't continue to grow. Make sure to overlap sheets of cardboard or newspaper so that no light gets through. If you're using newspapers, lay down a thick layer with 6–10 sheets. Water the cardboard or newspapers—this will help them conform to the ground better and will keep them from being blown away by wind.

2. Add Layers

After this, you can add an optional thin 1-inch (2.5 cm) layer of kitchen scraps, consisting of fruit and vegetable peels or waste, tea bags, coffee grounds, eggshells, and so on. Then you need to add a 2-inch (5 cm) layer of compost or manure, then a 3–4-inch (7.5–10 cm) layer of straw, then another 2-inch (5 cm) layer of compost or manure, and then a final 3–4-inch (7.5–10 cm) layer of straw. It's sensible to water each layer well before adding the next one. Your bed will compact as you water it. Aim to have it at least 6 inches (15 cm) tall after watering. You can continue layering it and have it taller than that if you'd like. Here are the layers of a no-dig garden bed in order:

1) Light-blocking material, like cardboard or newspapers
2) Kitchen scraps and food waste
3) Compost, manure, or a mix of both
4) Straw
5) Compost, manure, or a mix of both
6) Straw

You can add temporary wooden sides to your beds, and these will help keep your beds in shape for the first few months. This is not necessary, though. It's quicker and cheaper to make open-sided beds, and they will have fewer hiding places for slugs, ants, and woodlice. However, you must have weed-free paths between beds for this to work and absolutely no grass, which otherwise would invade beds with no sides.

If you have a lot of compost, the easiest way to create garden paths is to mulch them with compost. You can cover your whole garden area with cardboard or newspapers in order to prevent weeds and grass from growing, then you can create your garden beds, and then you need to simply mulch the garden paths between them with compost. You would need a 2-inch (5 cm) layer of compost for garden paths.

If you don't have a lot of compost, you can use other materials, like wood chips. Wood chips are cheap, and they break down with time, enriching your soil with nutrients. You need at least a 1-inch (2.5 cm) layer of wood chips, although I would suggest making it 2 inches (5 cm). You'll need to replace or top up the wood chips every few years.

3. Make Holes for Planting

Once you have these layers, you can create little indentations of 4 inches (10 cm) into the top layer of straw, fill them with compost, and then plant seeds or seedlings in there. By having these layers, you are creating the best growing medium for your plants as your plants are growing.

It's good to have a compost pile so that you have compost when you need it. Making your own compost is not difficult at all, and Chapter 6 has a section dedicated to making and using compost. The height of the original bed you make will shrink down as it breaks down—it will approximately halve in height in the first 6 months as it composts away, but you can add around 2 inches (5 cm) of mulch and top it up throughout the year to keep the soil full of nutrients. No-dig garden beds never need tilling or digging once they are established.

You can plant in no-dig garden beds right away. The cardboard will soften within 3 months, and plants will be able to root into the soil. However, it can be a good idea to plant shallow-rooted plants early on so that the cardboard and lower layers have time to decompose before planting deep-rooted plants. Cool-season crops, like lettuce, arugula, and radishes, are perfect for this. Later on, as the layers of materials break down further, you can plant deep-rooted plants, like peas, beans, tomatoes, squash, and more. Peas and beans also help enrich the soil with nitrogen, which will benefit the crops that are planted in later years.

Building Raised Beds

Raised beds work great in greenhouses and have quite a few benefits. They drain well and help prevent soil erosion. They also warm up more quickly in the springtime than regular garden beds. You have control over the soil you place in raised beds. Raised beds aren't as prone to weeds because they are elevated and you can fill them with weed-free soil. They also make tending to your garden more convenient because you don't have to bend down so far, so they are great for people with mobility issues.

If you'd like to build raised beds and you're wondering what kind of wood you should use, how large a raised bed should be, or how to clear a site and build a bed, this section of the book will help you.

A raised bed is essentially a frame box that has no top or bottom. You can build a raised bed without a frame—it can be a mound of soil—but I personally prefer framed raised beds to keep everything in place and stop the sides from crumbling and expanding.

Raised beds can look attractive and neat too. Having raised beds makes it very easy to separate and rotate crops. Raised beds are great for greenhouses and work well with the no-dig method. The minimum size for a raised bed is usually 4x4 feet (1.2x1.2 m), and they should be a minimum of 6 inches (15 cm) tall, but they'll need to be taller for plants that have a deeper root structure—18 inches (45 cm) is usually enough for most plants.

You can make raised beds using anything you have on hand: wood, stones, bricks, or cement blocks. Avoid treated wood because chemicals from it could leach into your soil. If you choose pine, it is inexpensive but may rot after a few years. You can get rot-resistant wood, like cedar or redwood, but it's more expensive. You can also use railroad ties or pallets. Concrete may increase the pH of the soil over time. Cinder blocks are a great material for building raised beds and will retain heat too. Rocks and stones work too, and they look great.

Raised beds should not be wider than 4 feet (1.2 m) so that you can easily reach everywhere without having to step on them. If you're putting a raised bed against a wall of your greenhouse, you might want it to be only 2–3 feet (60–90 cm) wide since you can only access it from one side. Length is not as important. You can make a bed that is 4x4 feet (1.2x1.2 m), 4x8 feet (1.2x2.4 m), or 4x12 feet (1.2x3.6 m). It can be as long as you want, but I personally find it easier to have multiple shorter beds rather than one really long bed. However, depending on the layout of your greenhouse, having a longer bed might be a practical solution.

How deep your raised beds should be depends on what plants you want to grow. Shallow-rooted plants, such as lettuce, leafy greens, spinach, onions, leeks, chives, radishes, strawberries, basil, dill, mint, cilantro (coriander), parsley, thyme, oregano, and marigolds, need a minimum soil depth of 6 inches (15 cm). Deep-rooted crops, such as carrots, beets, beans, broccoli, Brussels sprouts, cabbage, cauliflower, cucumbers, melons, garlic, kale, Swiss chard, turnips, potatoes, parsnips, squash, rosemary, sage, borage, lavender, and nasturtiums, need a minimum soil depth of 12 to 18 inches (30–45 cm). If you want to grow peppers, tomatoes, okra, eggplants, pumpkins, watermelons, or winter squash, they need the soil to have a depth of 18 inches (45 cm). If plants don't have loose soil to this depth, the roots won't be able to go down deep enough to access nutrients.

Usually, lumber comes in a standard size that is 6 inches (15 cm) in height. You can stack several boards to make your beds 12 or 18 inches (30 or 45 cm) tall or even taller. But keep in mind that the added weight of the soil will add pressure to the sides. You'll need to add cross-supports to any bed that is over 12 inches (30 cm) tall.

You'll need to prepare the area where you plan to build a raised bed before building it. Here's what basic site preparation for a raised bed looks like. First, outline the spot where you plant to build your raised bed. If you have grass in the area, mow it short, and dig out the clumps. Loosen the soil in the bed, flip the clumps of sod upside down, and add them to the bed. You can scrape the soil from the pathway around the outside and add that to the bed too.

You can also use the no-dig method to build raised beds, which I personally prefer. Mow the grass or weeds as close to the ground as possible. Then cover the area with cardboard or newspapers, which will smother the grass and weeds and eventually rot down into the soil as well. Be sure to overlap the cardboard or newspapers by about 6 inches (15 cm) to make sure no weeds slip through cracks. Next, add 6 inches (15 cm) of compost on top of the cardboard. If your raised bed will be 6 inches (15 cm) tall, the compost will be your growing medium. But if it will be taller, you'll need to fill the bed with topsoil and other materials, and the compost will go on top of that.

You can plant your raised beds right after setting them up. By the time the roots reach the cardboard, it will have started to break down, and the roots will be able to grow deeper below that cardboard layer. You can top up your raised beds with an inch or two (2.5–5 cm) of compost each fall or winter. This will help improve the quality and fertility of the soil not only in your raised beds but below them too.

How to Build a Raised Bed

Building a raised bed is not difficult at all and requires minimal DIY skills. You are essentially building a box with no top and bottom. Most lumber stores can cut the planks for you. Here's what you'll need to build a raised bed:

Tools

- Drill/driver and bits
- Screwdriver
- Hand saw and tape measure if cutting the planks yourself

Materials

- For a 4x8-foot (1.2x2.4 m) bed, get 3 pieces of 8-foot (2.4 m) long 2x6 in. (5x15 cm) lumber. If you can get 2x8 in. (5x20 cm) or 2x10 in. (5x25 cm) lumber, that's even better. For a 4x4-foot (1.2x1.2 m) bed, get 2 pieces of lumber. This will make a 6-inch-tall (15 cm) bed if you get 2x6 in. (5x15 cm) planks. If you want a taller bed, you'll need to double the amount of planks for a 12-inch-tall (30 cm) bed and triple it for an 18-inch-tall (45 cm) bed.

- You can get pine stakes for extra bracing.
- If you don't have a saw, ask the guys at the lumber yard to cut the pieces in half. For a 4x8-foot (1.2x2.4 m) bed, cut one of the pieces in half, which will give you two 4-foot (1.2 m) lengths to use for the ends. For a 4x4-foot (1.2x1.2 m) bed, cut both pieces in half.

Deck/Exterior Screws

To make your bed stronger, use a piece of 2x4 in. (5x10 cm) or 4x4 in. (10x10 cm) lumber in the corners to give you something stable to nail or screw into rather than the end grain of the board.

And here's how you build a raised bed:

1. If your 8-foot-long (2.4 m) boards were not pre-cut at the lumber store, mark off the half way point, and cut as many planks as you need for the 4-foot (1.2 m) sides of the bed.
2. Screw the planks together using decking screws. Two holes at the end of each plank is enough. Drill pilot holes using a drill bit slightly thinner than the screws themselves. One end of each plank will overlap the end of the next and screw directly into it, so position your pilot holes correspondingly. It will be easier if you have a helper to hold it while you fasten the corners.
3. If you'd like extra bracing and a sturdier frame, cut your pine stake into 4 pieces, and use them to nail the boards at the corners for bracing.
4. With all the wood cut to size and the holes drilled, you can start putting the bed together.
5. Lay down the bed. The walls need to be laid out so that each plank overlaps the next with the pilot holes located at the overlapping end.
6. Screw the walls together with long screws so that each wall is properly secured to the next.
7. Congratulations, you've just built your raised bed, and it's ready to be filled!

You could decide to bury the base of your raised bed slightly to stop weeds from encroaching. You can make your raised bed last longer by putting a heavy plastic liner inside the boards. You could put hardware cloth at the base of your raised beds if you're putting them on soil to prevent things like gophers and moles from getting into them.[6]

Now it's time to fill your raised beds. If you opted for the no-dig method and your beds are 6 inches (15 cm) tall, you can fill them with compost and use it as the growing medium. If your beds are taller, you'll need to fill them with other materials.

You can fill your raised beds with topsoil and then top it off with 6 inches (15 cm) of compost. If you want to know how much soil your raised beds require, you can use the formula of length x width x depth, and

---

[6] Image from https://www.themarthablog.com/2020/09/preparing-the-vegetable-greenhouse-beds-for-planting.html

this will give you how much soil you need in cubic feet or cubic meters.

Apart from just topsoil and compost, you can add things like vermiculite, worm castings, coconut coir, peat moss, and grass clippings. Below you will find a recipe for mixing soil for raised beds. I've been using it for years, and we've gotten some of the best harvests using this mix. It's a bit more complicated but definitely worth it. The amounts are for one 4x4-foot (1.2x1.2 m) raised bed. You can multiply the amounts for larger beds.

- 4 cubic feet (113 L) of topsoil
- 3 cubic feet (85 L) of coconut coir (you can use peat moss instead)
- 2–3 cubic feet (56.5–85L) of compost or composted manure
- 2-inch (5 cm) layer of shredded leaves or grass clippings

If you use grass clippings, make sure they are not from a lawn that has been sprayed with herbicides or been fertilized with food that contains granular herbicides to kill weeds. They both persist and will kill plants up to 3 years after the initial application. Simply mix all the materials with a hoe or a cultivator and water well. Now you're ready to fill your raised beds. If you use this recipe, you probably won't need to fertilize your raised beds much in the first year. But in the following years, you can add an inch or two (2.5–5 cm) of compost.

Checking and Changing Soil pH Level

You can get soil tests done where you check the pH level of your soil to see if it is acidic or alkaline. You can purchase pH testing kits online or at your local garden center. The instructions are easy to follow, and you will likely have to mix a sample of your soil with water and other ingredients and then dip a test strip in the solution. If the pH level is outside of the range, you may need to adjust it by using amendments.

The pH scale ranges from 0 to 14. The lower end of the scale is acidic, and the higher end is alkaline. The middle point—7.0—is neutral. Most plants prefer to grow in soil with a pH level between 6.0 and 7.5. Few plants, such as blueberries, need acidic soil with a pH level between 4 and 5.5.

You can use sulfur or aluminum sulfate to lower the pH level of your soil (make it more acidic). You can also use peat moss or fresh pine needles to make your soil more acidic, but these are usually not as effective and don't work as quickly as sulfur or aluminum sulfate. To increase the pH level of your soil (make it less acidic), you can add finely ground agricultural limestone. The amounts of sulfur, aluminum sulfate, or lime should be carefully measured before adding, so I would suggest checking with your local garden center—they should be able to help you with that.

I remember when I first prepared the garden beds in my first greenhouse (which was actually a hoop house) for planting. I marked the garden beds and started preparing the area by putting down cardboard on the grass, then compost, vegetable scraps, straw, more compost, and more straw. I made indentations in the beds, filled them with compost, and planted seedlings in there that I had grown from seed in containers 8 weeks earlier. We also had raised beds in another greenhouse later on, and I actually maintain them to this day.

Key takeaways from this chapter:

1. You don't have to dig or till the soil in your greenhouse. Instead, you can use the no-dig method, which aims to keep soil disturbance to a minimum, like in nature. It relies on using organic matter to feed the soil and help with drainage and aeration. It is easier for you and better for the environment. You can layer cardboard, newspapers, scraps, straw, and compost or manure to make no-dig garden beds.

2. Raised beds are a great choice for greenhouses. With raised beds, you can choose what soil to put in there. There will be no soil compaction. You won't have to bend or kneel. They need to be at least 6 inches (15 cm) tall, but they can be up to 18 inches (45 cm) tall for plants that have deeper roots. You can put hardware cloth at the bottom of raised beds to prevent moles and gophers from getting into them.

3. You can get soil tests done where you check the pH level of your soil and then adjust it if necessary. You can use sulfur or aluminum sulfate to lower the pH level of your soil (make it more acidic). To increase the pH level of your soil (make it less acidic), you can add finely ground agricultural limestone. The amounts of sulfur, aluminum sulfate, or lime should be carefully measured before adding, so I would suggest checking with your local garden center—they should be able to help you with that.

The next chapter will look at seeding and transplanting, and it will cover selecting and germinating seeds as well as transplanting your seedlings into bigger pots and eventually to garden beds to grow and thrive. It will also cover propagating plants from cuttings, which allows you to clone existing plants.

Chapter 5: Seeding and Transplanting

This chapter will cover everything you need to know about seeding and transplanting. Now that you have prepared your garden beds, it's time to move on to planting them with lovely vegetables that will produce an abundance of delicious produce for you and your family.

This chapter will cover how you select and start seeds and how you grow and transplant seedlings. It will also cover how you can maximize your growing space using intercropping and companion planting techniques, plus how you can propagate plants from cuttings. Planting a garden is one of my favorite parts of gardening, and I never cease to be amazed at what wonderful things you can grow from seeds. It's enormously satisfying checking on your seeds progress daily and watching them transform first into seedlings, then into plants, and finally see them produce delicious vegetables that can feed you and your family and friends. All home-grown organically and naturally without any chemicals, by you!

Selecting and Starting Seeds

Gardening would be super expensive if you were to buy all your plants as already established. Generally, the more established a plant is, the more expensive it is to buy because of all the work that has gone into getting it to that state. It is much cheaper to grow your own plants from seed. Growing plants from seed is not difficult, and it's so rewarding and enjoyable to see your plants grow from seed to finally gathering harvest from them. I can still remember the very first time I grew tomatoes from seed. Checking on their progress is one of the first things I did every day, and I bored my family and friends with constant updates on how they did, but I was so proud and excited to have grown actual plants from seed.

Ensure that you buy your seeds from a reputable company. I strongly suggest getting organic seeds. Organic seeds are seeds taken from plants grown without the use of synthetic fertilizers and pesticides, which means they are better for you and for the environment. Plants grown from organic seeds are also naturally better at fending off pests on their own.

Check the seed packet to see if the plants you want to grow would grow well in your location. You could look for regionally based companies with seeds that thrive in your area. Regional suppliers are less likely to offer seeds that are unsuited to your growing conditions.

When you are choosing vegetables to plant, do look on the back of seed packets or in the seed catalog for seeds that have characteristics of being disease resistant because this will give you better quality vegetables and may reduce pests that come into your garden. While you can keep seeds for a few years, it is preferable to buy new seeds each year to ensure you get a better crop.

Also, check the seed packet for details about the best time to sow them and what conditions the plants like to grow in. Most seed packets will tell you if they should be started indoors or sown directly in the garden. They will usually tell you how long it will take for the plants to produce edible produce (days to maturity), and they should tell you their light and water requirements. Some may give information about the type of soil the plant likes.

Make a list of the vegetables and herbs that you enjoy eating, and then think about where these would grow in your greenhouse. If you're a complete beginner to gardening, I would suggest starting out with vegetables that are easy to grow. Lettuce, green beans, peas, radishes, carrots, cucumbers, kale, Swiss chard, beets, and zucchini are all relatively easy to grow. Tomatoes and peppers require a bit more care, but they are not terribly difficult to grow. Eggplants, cauliflower, celery, and watermelons can be more difficult to grow.

If you don't like certain vegetables, don't grow them because if you don't enjoy eating them—it'll probably be just wasted time and food unless you plan to sell them. Remember that if you're growing peas, pole beans, cucumbers, tomatoes, or other vining plants, you'll need to have trellises to support them when they grow, and also remember that they may create shade as they grow, so take this into consideration. If you're planting pumpkins and watermelons, they need a lot of space to spread.

You can start seeds in containers in your greenhouse (or indoors if it's too cold) so that your seedlings are ready to be transplanted to garden beds either in your greenhouse or in your garden when the weather is warmer. Seed packets may say things like "plant inside 6 to 8 weeks before last frost". The last frost date refers to the average final spring frost in your area. Since you're growing in a greenhouse, it's not really relevant, and you should consider the temperature in your greenhouse instead. To germinate seeds, you'll need interior temperatures to be in the 65–75°F (18–24°C) range during the day and no lower than 50°F (10°C) during the night. Most seeds won't germinate if the temperature falls below 50°F (10°C).

Last frost dates can be important if you're going to transplant seedlings outside into the garden. These dates are only an estimate based on historical climate data and are not set in stone. In the US, the National Weather Service tracks this data and has created charts that show the average last frost dates for various areas. You can find them by simply going online and typing in the phrase "last frost date by zip", and you'll find websites where you can check the last frost date for your specific zip code.

You would typically start seeds in a seed starting tray or in small containers and then transplant the seedlings into bigger containers when they grow too big before finally transplanting them to your garden beds.

Some plants can be started indoors and then be transplanted to garden beds. Plants that can be started indoors include artichoke, basil, broccoli, Brussels sprouts, cabbage, cauliflower, celery, chard, chives, collard greens, eggplants, kale, leeks, mustard, parsley, peppers, and tomatoes.

Some plants don't transplant well and should be planted directly into the soil (this is called direct sowing). Plants that should be started directly in the soil include beans, beets, carrots, corn, garlic, okra, parsnips, pumpkins, radishes, squash, turnips, watermelons, and zucchini.

Some vegetables are grown from root divisions or bulbs. Some examples include asparagus, garlic, horseradish, onions, potatoes, rhubarb, and sweet potatoes.

This will be covered in more detail in Chapter 9 in individual plant profiles.

You can grow seeds in any containers, and this could be a good way to recycle butter or margarine tubs or yogurt pots. The container needs to be 2–3 inches (5–7.5 cm) deep with some drainage—you can simply poke a drainage hole at the bottom. You can also purchase seed starting trays especially for this purpose, and it does make transplanting seedlings easier when you need to.

You can start seeds in potting mix, but most seeds, especially smaller ones, do better when started in seed starting mix, and it should be a fresh, sterile mix. I would advise against starting seeds in potting soil and especially in garden soil because this can lead to fungal diseases and kill your seeds. Seed starting mix is a special form of soilless potting mix that typically uses smaller particles of vermiculite and sand and omits organic materials found in standard potting soil. You can loosen and dampen the seed starting mix before planting seeds, but don't soak it. If you start seeds in seed starting mix, you'll generally need to transplant the seedlings into a standard potting mix or potting soil when they begin to develop into larger plants.

You can make your own seed starting mix by mixing equal parts of coco coir, perlite, and vermiculite. Simply combine all the ingredients in a clean tub or bucket, and water the mixture well. Stir the mixture with your hands or a trowel until it's moist but not soggy (like a wrung-out sponge). You can fill your seed starting trays or pots with this mix and sow your seeds right away.

You can also make your own potting mix for transplanting your seedlings into when they grow. You can make a basic potting mix or an enriched one with compost. To make a basic potting mix, mix 6 parts coco coir, 1 part perlite, and 1 part vermiculite. Enriched potting mix is made by mixing 4 parts coco coir, 2 parts compost, 1 part perlite, and 1 part vermiculite. Simply combine all the ingredients in a clean tub or bucket, and water the mixture well. Then stir it until it's moist but not soggy.

Look at the packet instructions diligently for how deep you should plant your seeds. Some small seeds just need to be scattered over the surface of the soil, while others need to be planted in a hole. If you don't have a dibber (a tool for making holes to plant seeds into), you can simply use an old pencil to make a hole, drop the seed in, and then cover it with soil if you're sowing directly or seed starting mix if you're starting seeds in containers. It's a good idea to plant 2–3 seeds per hole because not every seed you plant will germinate. There isn't anything you're doing wrong—it's just nature.

If more than one seed grows, you can thin them out. It simply means you should let the strongest looking one grow and cut the rest at the base. You should thin out seedlings when they have developed 1–2 true leaves. The very first leaves that plants grow from seed are called seed leaves or cotyledons. They are long and narrow in some plants, but in others, they are heart shaped. True leaves come after seed leaves. They have the same shape as the adult foliage, just baby sized.

You will need to keep the soil or seed starting mix moist but not soggy. You would typically need to water your seeds daily, and you can spray your seed starting mix with a spray bottle if you're starting seeds in containers, or you can spray the soil with a fine spray hose nozzle or water it with a watering can if you're direct sowing seeds in garden beds.

If you're starting seeds in containers, you can keep the seeds covered with a clear plastic dome or wrap, and this will help them to germinate more quickly. You can purchase heating mats to germinate seeds because most seeds germinate well in temperatures between 65 and 75°F (18–24°C). Your seeds will need to be watered more if you use a heating mat. You could also place a fan near them to improve air circulation.

Once the seedlings emerge, remove the plastic dome or wrap you had covering them. When the seedlings have started to grow, keep watering them the same way. Keep the soil or seed starting mix moist but not soggy—it should feel like a damp sponge. You would typically need to water your seedlings daily.

Seedlings need lots of light, which should not be a problem in a greenhouse. However, in the winter the days are short and the weather can be cloudy, so seedlings can start to get long and leggy because they reach for the light, but this will make them weaker. The same can happen if you're growing them indoors, as they might not get enough light from the windowsill. The only way to prevent seedlings from becoming leggy is to provide more light. You can do that by getting grow lights for your seedlings.

Having adequate lighting is essential for growing seedlings successfully. You would typically use fluorescent or LED (light-emitting diode) grow lights for starting seeds. Metal halide (MH) and high-pressure sodium (HPS) lights produce lots of heat and can burn seedlings. Fluorescent grow lights are cheaper than LEDs; however, LED grow lights have a few benefits over fluorescent grow lights. They are more energy efficient and last longer than fluorescent grow lights. They also don't lose their effectiveness over time.

If you get grow lights for seedlings, you shouldn't leave them on all day long. Seedlings need 8–10 hours of artificial light per day if they are getting some sunlight and 14–16 hours of light if they don't get any light or are grown indoors, so you should have your lights on a timer for convenience. Some people grow seedlings indoors with 12 hours of light daily, but it's usually not enough in my experience. You can try that, but you should monitor your seedlings closely in this case. If they start getting tall and growing sideways, you should add 2 more hours of light per day.

Issues with Seeds

If not all your seeds germinate, it's worth having another read of the back of the seed packet to see if you did everything it suggested in terms of temperature, light, and water. Have the seeds rotted because the soil was too moist? Or was the soil too dry, and the seeds dried out? Try again and try to follow the instructions and be consistent with how moist your soil is.

If your seedlings are tall, leggy, and spindly, it could be that they aren't getting enough light, so they're growing to try to reach the light. They should get 14–16 hours of bright light per day, which you can help along with grow lights. If the temperature is too warm, this can cause plants to be leggy too. If that's the case, you could reduce the temperature in the room and also use a little less fertilizer.

In the picture on the next page, it shows the difference between the seeds on the left, which were grown under grow lights, and the seeds on the right, which were grown on a windowsill and have become leggy.

If your seedlings looked good, and then suddenly they toppled at the base, this could be due to a soil-borne fungus known as damping off. Damping off can affect most seedlings, particularly under conditions of high humidity, poor air circulation, and if seeds were sown too thickly. It is mainly a problem when starting seeds in containers. Damping off is mainly caused by overly moist soil, which is ideal for the growth and spread of fungal pathogens.[7]

There is no cure for plants that have damping off. If you have it in the soil, I would recommend getting rid of it and using a soilless growing medium instead because you can't get rid of it once it's there. This is why I recommend using seed starting mix, which is a soilless growing medium, for starting seeds in the first place. Also, try not to overwater your seed starting mix, and sow the seeds more thinly because overcrowding can lead to damping off.

When I first tried to grow cucamelon seeds, I had this happen, and it was so frustrating to see little seeds starting to sprout and then just die for what seemed like no good reason. I then started using seed starting mix to start seeds and never had this problem again.

If you have mold growing on the surface of the seed starting mix or potting mix, this is a sign that the growing medium is too wet. It may not harm the plants too much, but definitely stop watering them for a few days, and you could put a fan nearby too, which will help with air circulation. You can scrape off the mold or put the seedlings in fresh potting mix, but be really careful and try not to damage them.[8]

Growing and Transplanting Seedlings

When you're growing seedlings, the growing medium needs to be kept moist but not soggy. The best indicator that your seeds or seedlings need water is how dry their growing medium is. When you touch the potting mix or soil, it should feel neither soggy nor too dry. Instead, it should feel like a moist sponge. When watering your seedlings, use a mister or a very gentle spray bottle to water the top of your seed starting tray or container. If you sowed seeds directly, you can water your seedlings carefully with a fine spray hose nozzle or a watering can. You should fertilize seedlings

---

[7] Image from https://www.gardeners.com/how-to/how-to-start-seeds/5062.html

[8] Image from https://www.thespruce.com/successful-start-seed-indoors-1402478

with an organic liquid fertilizer when they grow to 3 inches (7.5 cm) and then weekly after that.

One of the best ways to determine if a seedling is ready to be transplanted to a garden bed is to look at how many true leaves it has. The very first leaves that plants grow from seed are called seed leaves or cotyledons. They are long and narrow in some plants, but in others, they are heart shaped. True leaves come after seed leaves. They have the same shape as the adult foliage, just baby sized. You will need to wait until your seedlings have at least 3–4 true leaves before transplanting them to your garden beds.

However, if the weather is still too cold, you can continue growing seedlings in containers. You will have to pot them up as they grow, though. Potting up seedlings, whether you've grown them yourself or have purchased them from a nursery, just means putting them into larger containers so that they can grow and thrive. Seedlings need to be put into larger containers so that they have room for their roots to grow and don't become root bound.

If you haven't seen a root-bound plant before, the picture on the right shows what one looks like. This is a tomato seedling that has been in a small container much too long. You can see how the roots have just grown into the container shape because they had nowhere else to go.[9]

You can sometimes gently massage a root-bound plant before you transplant it into a bigger pot, but you need to be careful not to damage the roots when you do this.

When you pot up seedlings, their roots will become bigger and will take up more water. Seedlings are always very thirsty and need lots of water to thrive. When you've put seedlings into their new containers, do remember to feed them because they'll want to take in as many good nutrients as they can to grow strong.

You can plant seedlings when plants are starting to look cramped and overgrown in their small seed starting trays. If plants have started out in 4-inch (10 cm) pots, then around 6–8 weeks after germination they can be moved into 6–8-inch (15–20 cm) pots.

The time for transplanting seedlings into bigger pots can depend on the plant too. Tomatoes will outgrow their pots very quickly, but herbs can take a bit more time. Tomatoes grow faster than peppers, for example, so they will need to be planted sooner than peppers. Vegetables like squash grow fast and like a lot of room, so it can be fine to start squash in 6-inch (15 cm) pots.

If your seedlings are starting to have their roots poke out of drainage holes, this is a key sign that they need to be transplanted into larger containers. You can

---

[9] Image from https://homesteadandchill.com/potting-up-seedlings/

pot up seedlings before this happens, but this is just a sign they're definitely ready to be put into larger containers.[10]

One helpful tip when you're potting up seedlings is to make a "dummy hole" or placeholder with the existing container in the new container that the seedling is being transplanted into. You can fill the new container with potting soil, then place the existing container in it and check that things are at the right level. Ensure the soil in the new container is moist. When you do this, it will help ensure that there are no air pockets around the plant, and it saves you having to tip in extra soil, which can get all over the leaves of the plant and be a bit awkward. It also means that transplanting of the seedling goes smoothly and stops the plant from being jostled about. Prior to learning about this tip, we often had over- or underfilled containers and had to mess about with soil levels.

When it comes to transplanting seedlings to garden beds, simply poke a hole in the soil, carefully remove the seedling from its container trying not to disturb the roots, put the seedling into the hole you've made, firm the soil around it, and water it thoroughly.

Ensure that there is plenty of space between plants and between rows because plants need room to grow and spread out. This will also improve air circulation around the plants, which will help prevent fungal diseases. Crowding plants is a common mistake that gardeners make. If plants are too crowded and don't have enough space between them, it means they will compete for nutrients and space. While seedlings may seem small, they will become much larger as they grow, so do consider the space that mature plants need.

Different plants need different spacing. You can usually find spacing requirements for plants on seed packets. Plant profiles in Chapter 9 will cover spacing requirements for many different plants.

If you're transplanting seedlings outside into the garden, don't put them directly outside—the transition to being outside needs to be gradual. You can start by putting them in a protected place outdoors for a few hours while they are still in containers, but bring them back inside at night because it might be too cold for them. Over 10 days, gradually let them get used to

---

[10] Image from https://homesteadandchill.com/potting-up-seedlings/

being outside more and more. After that, you can transplant them into your garden. A cold frame is also a good place to harden off seedlings.

When you eventually reach the day when you transplant your seedlings into the garden, it could be a good idea to choose an overcast day to reduce the stress for the plants because if they've been in a greenhouse or indoors and then they are placed in the harsh outside world, it can be a shock. Ensure that you water them well, and it can be a good idea to add 2 inches (5 cm) of mulch to keep back the weeds and retain moisture (this will be covered in the next chapter in more detail).

Propagating Plants from Cuttings

If you're just starting out with vegetable gardening, you'll likely have to start plants from seed or purchase seedlings from a nursery. There is another way to start plants, however—from cuttings. It's exactly what it sounds like—you can use cuttings from existing plants to grow new plants. Taking cuttings from plants is a great way to propagate them. It is also called cloning. Some plants can be difficult to start from seed, so you can purchase a plant from a nursery and then propagate it via cuttings.

I have always adored taking plant cuttings. I love the fact that from one plant you can create numerous others and watch them grow. I do this with all my house plants, and I have done this with plants that I grow in my garden too.

When you propagate plants this way, often the parent plant has done a lot of the growing work, so new plants will grow much quicker than from seed. Only take cuttings from healthy, strong plants. Take a few more cuttings than required because sometimes not all of the cuttings survive.

Here's what you'll need to propagate plants from cuttings:

- Existing plant (parent plant)
- Razor blade or scissors
- Rubbing alcohol
- 4–6-inch (10–15 cm) containers or a seed starting tray
- Clear plastic cover for seed starting tray or a plastic bag
- Soilless potting mix
- Pencil or stick
- Rooting hormone
- Water
- 2 small plastic cups

You'll need a porous, soilless growing medium. You can make your own by mixing equal parts of sand, perlite, peat moss, and vermiculite. Do not add fertilizers or manure to this because they can burn cuttings.

You can start cuttings in seed starting trays, but larger plants may need a 4–6-inch (10–15 cm) deep container. You can also use Styrofoam coffee cups or large paper cups, but make sure to poke a drainage hole at the bottom.

Here's how you propagate plants from cuttings:

1. Choose a healthy parent plant to take cuttings from. Don't take cuttings from diseased or wilting plants. The parent plant should have good, green growth and be large enough to take cuttings from.
2. Next, fill your seed starting tray or container with the growing medium, and poke a hole in it with the pencil.

3. Now you'll need to find suitable stems for cutting. They should be green and non-woody. Newer growth is easier to root than older or woody stems. Find a stem with a node—a bump along the stem where a leaf or a flower bud attaches. New roots will emerge from it.

4. Sterilize your razor blade or scissors with rubbing alcohol, and make a clean cut just below the node. The cutting doesn't need to be long, 4–6 inches (10–15 cm) is enough, but it should have at least 2 leaves and 1 node.

5. Once you've taken the cutting, you need to make a partial slice through the middle of the node with a sterilized razor blade. This will increase the chances of roots emerging from this spot. If your cutting has more than 1 or 2 leaves—cut them off. The cutting only needs 1–2 leaves to continue photosynthesis. Having too many leaves will consume energy that would otherwise go to root creation. If the leaves are very large in relation to the stem, you can cut off the top halves of the leaves too.

6. Next, you'll need to dip the cutting in the rooting hormone. Rooting hormones are typically not organic; however, you can find organic options made with willow extract. I find gel or liquid rooting hormones to be more effective than powder. This step is optional, but rooting hormone can help promote root growth, and I would recommend doing it. Fill one plastic cup with water, and place some rooting hormone into the other one. Dip the node end of the cutting into the water and then into the rooting hormone. Tap off any excess hormone—too much can hinder the chances for successful rooting.

7. Carefully place the cutting into the hole you made in the growing medium, and gently tap the growing medium around the cutting. You can fit several cuttings into one container, but space them out so that the leaves don't touch one another.

8. Place the container with the cutting into a plastic bag, or cover the seed staring tray with a clear plastic cover. It will keep the humidity high and hold in heat. Don't seal the bag completely because cuttings need some airflow to prevent fungal rot. You can remove the cover from the seed starting tray once a day to let the moisture escape. Keep the cuttings in a warm, sunny spot, but don't put them in full sunlight until new leaves start to appear along the stem.

9. Keep the growing medium slightly moist but not so wet that condensation forms on the inside of the plastic bag or seed starting tray cover until the roots form. After 2–3 weeks, you can start checking for roots by tugging gently on the cutting. When you begin to feel resistance, it means the roots have developed. At this point, you can transplant the cutting into your garden.

You can grow a lot of different plants from cuttings, including tomatoes, peppers, celery, sweet potatoes, fennel, basil, rosemary, lemon verbena, lavender, mint, and more.

Maximizing Growing Space

Intercropping and companion planting are terms that are often used interchangeably, and while they both refer to growing different plants together, it's done for different reasons. Intercropping is done to maximize growing space. Some plants feed from different levels of the soil, so when you plant them together, they won't compete for nutrients, and you can maximize your growing space this way. Companion planting is when you grow plants together for the benefit of one or both of those plants. When some plants are grown together, they can help enhance each other's growth and protect each other from pests and diseases. This is something that you can do not only with vegetables but also herbs and flowers. It is a great thing to do if you want to make the most of your garden space and live in a sustainable way.

Your whole garden is a place of biodiversity, and both intercropping and companion planting can help improve it. There is a wide range of plants, animals, bacteria, and fungi that live in it, which are connected. Plants interact with one another, and they have beneficial relationships. Some plants will attract insects and pollinators that are beneficial for your garden. Others will repel pests and fend off animals that can eat or damage your crops. Legumes will enrich the soil with nitrogen, which will help other plants grow. And tall plants can provide shade and/or support for plants that need it.

Intercropping is typically done in rows where two or more crops are grown together and at least one of the crops is planted in rows. You can either plant the other crop between the rows or plant both plants in alternating rows to keep things more organized.

When intercropping, you should consider the growth rate of plants above and below the ground. Crops that root deeply, such as parsnips, carrots, and tomatoes, can be intercropped with vegetables that have shallow roots, such as broccoli, lettuce, and potatoes. Fast-growing plants, like spinach, can be tucked in around slow maturing plants, like corn. You can also take advantage of the shade provided by tall and broad leaf plants, like corn and sunflowers, and plant lettuce, spinach, or celery underneath.

As for companion planting, most herbs and flowers like marigolds and nasturtiums work well with virtually any plant. Marigolds and nasturtiums will help repel pests and attract lots of different beneficial insects (who will eat pests) and pollinators. Herbs, like basil, rosemary, mint, and others, repel a variety of different pests. However, do not plant fennel near your vegetables because it will stunt their growth. If you want to grow it, it's best to plant it away from other plants.

One of the best companion planting combinations is growing basil and tomatoes together. The smell of basil repels thrips and moths, which lay tomato hornworms. Basil also repels whiteflies from tomatoes and is said to improve the flavor of the tomatoes. So, this companion planting strategy will prevent your tomatoes from being attacked by pests.

Other combinations that work well include planting carrots, lettuce, and peas together or Brussels sprouts with onions and nasturtiums. Peas and carrots are ideal companions when you plant them in late summer for fall harvest. Both crops thrive in cool, moist conditions and mature in around 70 to 80 days. Brussels sprouts are great companions for onions and nasturtiums because they grow upright on their own pole, while onions form bulbs underground, and nasturtiums spread and their leaves give excellent cover, which helps keep the soil moist and prevent weeds.

Planting carrots and radishes together works well too because radishes grow quickly and can be harvested before carrots start to mature.

However, just like there are companion plants, there are also plants that don't grow well together. There is proper terminology to describe plants that are unfriendly to one another and don't make good companions—"allelopathy"—this means that a plant may impact the growth, survival, or development of another plant. Plants sometimes do this as a survival strategy because they want all the soil space and nutrients.

Fennel, as mentioned previously, is one of such plants, and it should be planted away from your other plants. It's also a good idea not to plant dill, cilantro (coriander), or any other members of the carrot family near carrots because they will stunt the growth of carrots. Also, don't plant garlic or onions near peas because peas will have stunted growth.

For companion planting to work, plants should be planted within 2–3 rows of each other. Plants that don't grow well together should be planted at least 2–3 rows apart.

If you plant companion plants in the same row and they have different spacing requirements, you can take an average spacing between the plants. If one plant needs 16 inches (40 cm) of space and the other needs 8 inches (20 cm), you can space them 12 inches (30 cm) apart. Remember to consider the height of your plants for proper shading. Try not to completely shade out any of your shorter plants.

While planting vegetables from the same family seems the logical thing to do, it's not always the best decision. Plants from the same family generally require the same growing conditions, but they also attract the same pests. Different plants families will be covered in Chapter 7 in the section on crop rotation.

I remember when I first bought and started seeds for my garden. I sowed carrots and beets directly because they are root crops and don't like being transplanted, and I started tomatoes, basil, and peppers, among other things, in containers in my greenhouse because they like warmth and I wanted to get a head start on the growing season by starting them early in containers. It's an incredible process all along, from buying packets of seeds at a garden center or online to watching the seeds sprout, grow, and get bigger and stronger, then transplanting the little seedlings into garden beds and watching the plants grow, and then eventually seeing these plants flower and fruit. You can hardly believe it—it feels magical.

Key takeaways from this chapter:

1. Seeds are less expensive than seedlings or established plants. Ensure the seeds you use are organic, fresh, and are from a reputable company.
2. Plant seeds for vegetables that you would like to eat and that you know grow well in your area.
3. Use trellises to support climbing or vining plants.
4. Some plants do better when started in containers, whereas others don't like to be transplanted and are better sown directly.
5. You can get disease-resistant seed varieties.
6. You can start seeds in your greenhouse or indoors before the growing season starts and then transplant them into garden beds in your greenhouse or into the garden outside in order to get a head start on the growing season.

7. Grow seeds in seed starting mix that is sterile and contains no organic materials to avoid fungal issues.

8. Cover seeds with a plastic dome or plastic wrap. Remove the cover once the seedlings have emerged.

9. You'll need to water your seeds daily and keep the soil or seed starting mix moist but not too wet. Once they sprout, you can water the seedlings daily too. You can give your seedlings liquid fertilizer once they are at least 3 inches (7.5 cm) tall.

10. You can use grow lights to provide more light for your seedlings. Keep them on for 14–16 hours a day on a timer.

11. When seedlings have 3–4 sets of true leaves, they are ready to be transplanted to garden beds. If you're transplanting them into the garden outside, transition to the outside should be gradual. You can move your seedlings outside during the day while they're still in containers, but bring them back inside at night. Do so for 10 days before planting your seedlings outside. Cold frames are great for hardening your seedlings.

12. Transplant seedlings into your garden on an overcast day so that it is less stressful for them.

13. Give seedlings space and think about their size when they are fully grown.

14. You can also start plants from cuttings (which is also called cloning), and it's a great way to propagate plants.

15. Companion planting can provide benefits for your plants when they are grown together, while intercropping can help you maximize your growing space.

The next chapter will cover everything you need to know to maintain your garden properly, looking at how to water it and maintenance tasks you need to do to keep your plants healthy and producing a good quality crop and to keep your garden looking its best.

Chapter 6: Maintaining Your Greenhouse Garden

Once you've started your greenhouse garden, it does need some care and maintenance to ensure that your plants thrive. You will need to water your plants, keep your garden free from weeds, and mulch the soil to provide nutrients and keep the weeds down. You will also need to prune some plants. It is important to follow the guidance for care on the back of each seed packet. Your greenhouse will also need some maintenance and cleaning from time to time. So, this chapter will cover everything you need to know about maintaining your garden and your greenhouse.

Watering

How Much You Should Water Your Plants

People can be unsure about how much water they should give their plants and how often they should water them. Watering your garden can depend on the type of soil you have, the climate you live in, the time of year, and the type of plants you are growing.

Having an outside source of water really eases the pressure of having to carry watering cans through your house. And you'll need a lot of watering cans even if you have a small garden. So, if you have access to an outside tap, this is a treasure! If you have a well, you could hook a hose directly to the well for watering. If you don't have an outside tap or a well, you could consider getting a water butt. It's not that expensive, and it will collect lots of delicious rainwater to feed your plants, which they'll love. It would also help you save on your water bill, so it's a win-win situation. If you don't have either of these, you could think about running a hose from a tap in your house out to the greenhouse. Hose reels are very easy to manage. They're convenient and don't take up a lot of space and will make life much easier.

Most plants should ideally get an inch or two (2.5–5 cm) of water each week, and they prefer good, deep watering rather than frequent, shallow watering. When you water more often but not as deeply, you get weak root growth and evaporation. Therefore, watering your garden beds about 1–2 inches (2.5–5 cm) or so once a week is preferable. Most plants typically need 1 inch (2.5 cm) of water per week, although during peak summer you should increase that to 2 inches (5 cm). To determine when you need to water your plants, you can simply place your finger about an inch (2.5 cm) into the soil, and if it feels dry, you need to water it.

An inch of water is a 1-inch-deep (2.5 cm) layer of water over the entire soil surface in question. Since you're growing in a greenhouse, your plants won't get any water from rain. To measure the volume of water your garden needs, you can simply multiply your garden beds' length by width in inches or centimeters and then by 1 or 2 inches (2.54–5.08 cm, but you can round that up to 2.5–5 cm for convenience) depending on how much water your garden needs. Next, divide the result by 231 if your measurements were in inches or by 1000 if they were in centimeters to get the number of gallons or liters of water your garden needs, respectively. For example, if you have a 4x8-foot garden bed, and your garden needs an inch of water, multiply 48 by 96 by 1, then divide by 231 to determine how many gallons you need. The answer would be 19.95 (you can round that up to 20 for convenience). Or let's say you have a 1.2 by 2.4 m garden bed that needs 2.5 cm of water. You'll need to multiply 120 by 240 by 2.5, then divide by 1000 to determine how many liters you need. In this case, your garden will need 72 liters of water.

When You Should Water Your Plants

First of all, you should water plants once you plant them. For already established gardens, watering them once a week with 1 or 2 inches (2.5–5 cm) of water is OK. However, if the weather is really hot, you may need to water them more frequently—twice a week or even more is the heat scorching. Some vegetables are thirstier and dry out quicker too. In my experience, tomatoes need a lot of water, and their soil can dry out quickly. You can check how moist your soil is by simply placing your finger about an inch (2.5 cm) into the soil. If it feels dry, you need to water it.

When you water your plants, you should aim to water them near the base. Watering your garden in the morning is best. Plants absorb moisture more effectively in the morning and become hydrated before the weather heats up. If you water your plants in the morning, this allows any water that may get on leaves to dry or evaporate throughout the day rather than just sit there overnight. If your plants remain wet for extended periods of time, this can lead to fungal diseases. Another thing that can happen if you water your plants in the midday sun and get water on the leaves, the water droplets can act like a magnifying glass and scorch the leaves of your plants.

What Happens if Plants Don't Get Enough Water?

If your plants don't get enough water, this is known as drought stress, and this can cause your plants to produce small fruit or none at all. Vegetables like cabbage and turnips can become tough, bitter, or fibrous. Some may have a flower stalk but then not grow anymore. Or plants could just have wilted leaves, shrivel up, and die.

You can look for signs that plants are underwatered. If they have dry, brown leaf edges, slow leaf growth, leaf curl, yellow leaves, wilted leaves, or branch dieback, these are all signs they may need more water. If your plants look dry or look like they're suffering from heat, water them. Leafy greens, such as lettuce, kale, and spinach, have shallow root systems and don't hold moisture well, so they do need to be watered regularly to thrive.

What Happens if Plants Get Too Much Water?

It is possible to overwater plants, and this often leads to root rot. Roots need oxygen from the soil, but if it's saturated with water, there's not enough oxygen there. Plants can collapse or have bland fruit if that's the case. If you are growing vegetables with the intention of storing them, they won't store well if they've been overwatered often—this applies to potatoes, onions, winter squash, and rutabaga.

You can check for signs that a plant is overwatered. If plants look wilted, have brown leaves or yellow falling leaves, if new growth is dropping off, or if a plant is floppy, slimy, or has smelly roots (which is a sign of root rot), this means your plants are likely overwatered.

Drip Irrigation

While watering your plants can be a relaxing experience, it can take quite a bit of time and effort, especially if you have a bigger garden. You can make watering less of a chore by installing a drip irrigation system. Drip irrigation is the most effective way of watering your plants in my opinion. Drip irrigation lines water the soil at an even rate, and you're not wasting water like with sprinklers due to evaporation.

Drip irrigation is a great solution because it helps prevent diseases by minimizing water contact with the leaves, stems, and fruit of plants. It also allows the rows between plants to remain dry, improving access and reducing weed growth. Drip irrigation systems will help you save time, money, and water because they are incredibly efficient.

You can buy drip irrigation kits from garden centers or home improvement/hardware stores. Many kits are modular in design, which allows you to change your drip irrigation system as your garden changes. I would suggest making a plan of your greenhouse layout and taking it to a store so that they can suggest a kit that would fit your needs best. Drip irrigation kits are relatively affordable and are not very difficult to install, so you can certainly do it yourself, or you can always hire someone to install the system for you.

Watering Raised Beds

Watering raised beds is essentially the same as watering regular garden beds. You can water your raised beds using a watering can, a garden hose, or drip lines. Watering raised beds with a watering can is can take quite a lot of effort and be time consuming. A garden hose would speed up the process, but don't blast young plants with a hose because this can damage them. You can also place a hose on the soil and let water drain into your raised beds. The soil should never become fully dry in your raised beds. Keep an eye on the weather because your plants may need more (if it's hot) or less water (if it's cold) as it changes.

Drip Irrigation for Raised Beds

You can get drip irrigation kits for raised beds. Just like with in-ground gardens, this is a great solution for watering your plants. If you have an automatic watering system, it's a good idea to let it water when you are naturally in the garden so that you can check that it's working correctly and there aren't any issues, like a dead battery, a faulty timer, or leaks, and that your raised beds are not being over- or underwatered. Raised beds should be watered evenly and consistently, which is why an automatic watering system can be a good idea.

Mulching

Mulching means covering the soil with a layer of mulch, which is any material that is spread or laid over the surface of the soil and used for a covering. Mulching helps retain moisture in the soil, reduce weeds, keep the soil and plants' roots cool in the summer and warm in the winter, and make garden beds and raised beds look more attractive.

You can use different materials for mulching. Some are more aesthetically pleasing than others, while others are more functional and can add nutrients to the soil. There are two categories of mulch: organic and inorganic, and both have their advantages and disadvantages. Organic mulch is made of natural materials. It will decompose over time and add beneficial nutrients to your soil. It can reduce weeds, but it doesn't always fully block weeds. Inorganic mulch is made of synthetic materials. It can fully block weeds, and it's better at retaining moisture than organic mulch, but it won't add nutrients to the soil. No-dig gardening uses organic mulch.

Organic mulch materials include compost, shredded leaves, wood chips, pine needles, straw, grass clippings, newspapers, peat moss, and coconut coir. As mentioned previously, organic mulch will decompose, so it will need to be replaced after some time. But while it's decomposing, it will add nutrients to the soil as well as help improve the soil structure, texture, and drainage. The drier and woodier the mulch, the slower it will decompose and the fewer nutrients it will give to the soil.

Wood chips and straw are commonly used for mulching in no-dig gardening. These are both great options, as they are relatively affordable and easy to spread. I personally like using compost as mulch. It's one of the best materials for mulching, and it's commonly used with the no-dig method. If you have a compost pile and lots of compost, you can use it for mulching, but wood chips or straw would work just fine too.

If you decide to use pine needles, keep in mind they can reduce the pH level of the soil and make it slightly more acidic, but usually not enough to cause any problems to plants. Also, make sure to use needles that have been dried, or they can rot and cause mold to grow otherwise. Most newspapers should be fine to use for mulching because they use soy-based black inks and hydrogen peroxide for bleaching pulp. But don't use glossy magazines or newspapers with colored or glossy inks because they may contain chemicals that are toxic to plants.

Inorganic mulch materials include plastic or landscape fabric and gravel or stone. Inorganic mulch materials are good at holding in moisture and blocking weeds. Since they don't decompose, they don't add any nutrients to the soil, but at the same time they don't need to be replaced as often as organic mulches.

You can mulch both garden beds and raised beds. Don't add mulch if you've just planted the seeds. The best time to mulch your garden is when the seedlings are at least 3–5 inches (7.5–12.5 cm) tall.

To mulch your garden, simply place your chosen mulch material on the soil, but keep it 3 inches (7.5 cm) away from the base of plants. Make sure the mulch is dry, and it should be in small pieces. Mulch should be placed on top of the soil but not in it because this will prevent your plants' roots from getting enough water, air, and nutrients they need for healthy growth. You would typically need a 2–3-inch (5–7.5 cm) layer of mulch for it to be effective. Make sure the mulch doesn't touch the leaves of your plants because this can spread diseases.

When you water mulched garden beds or raised beds, aim the water at the base of plants. If you pour water directly on the mulch, it may lead to water retention and root rot. Drip irrigation works great with mulched gardens.

If you're not using your garden beds to grow plants (for example, if it's too cold) you can leave the mulch, as it will decompose and enrich your soil with nutrients. When mulch seems to be too dry and brittle, you'll need to remove it and replace it with fresh material. Straw breaks down rather quickly and typically needs to be topped up every year. Wood chips are a bit more durable and can last up to 2 years. If mulch becomes too compacted and starts blocking water flow to the roots, again, you'll need to replace it. If you notice any fungi or any signs of diseases on your plants, you'll need to remove your mulch, bag it up, and dispose of it in the trash. Some pests can use mulch as shelter, and if you notice pests in mulched areas of your garden, you can turn the mulch with a rake or spray it with an organic pesticide. If that doesn't help, you'll need to replace it.

Also, don't forget to maintain your garden paths. If you have them covered with straw, wood chips, compost, or other material, make sure to top them up too because these materials will break down with time, just like mulch on your garden beds does.

Managing Weeds In and Around the Greenhouse

You might think that weeds can't get to your greenhouse since you're essentially growing plants in an enclosed space, but that's not true. Weeds and their seeds can be brought into a greenhouse on infested plant material, tools, equipment, animals, and people. Seeds can be moved by wind, irrigation water, and by seeds being naturally propelled.

When weeds grow near your vegetables, they will compete with them for sunlight, water, and nutrients. You want your vegetables to get all the benefits of sunlight, water, and nutrients so that they grow strong and healthy and taste delicious. You need to pull up weeds weekly to stop them from developing thick and deep roots if you see them growing in your greenhouse. It is also important to control weeds around the greenhouse to prevent them from getting inside it.

In no-dig gardening, mulching is used to control weeds, and it's a great technique for controlling weeds in the greenhouse. If mulch areas have thinned, you could top them up, and the mulch will prevent weeds from growing and will also help retain moisture in the soil.

However, you might still get a few weeds here and there. There are a few different ways to remove them, which include hand weeding, shallow hoeing, and using contact weed killers.

Hand weeding is self-explanatory—it means simply pulling the weeds up with your hands. It's an effective method of weed control, but it can take quite a bit of time and effort, especially if you have a larger garden.

Shallow hoeing is hoeing that "fluffs" the soil on the surface. Stirrup hoes (shuffle hoes) are ideal for shallow hoeing. Shallow hoeing works on newly germinated weeds. It kills them and stirs up the weed seed in the top ½ inch (1.2 cm) of the soil. "Fluffing" the soil makes it harder for the next bunch of weed seeds to germinate.

Contact weed killers are organic herbicides that kill weeds on contact. Organic options are non-selective, however, which means they will kill any plant they touch, so you should be careful when applying them. They work best on annual weeds (the ones that complete their lifecycle in a year). They are not as effective against perennial weeds (the ones that die back seasonally but grow back in the spring), but they can weaken them after repeated applications. They typically come in liquid form, either pre-diluted or as concentrates that you need to dilute yourself. You simply need to spray a weed killer on the leaves and stems of weeds for it to work. As mentioned previously, organic contact weed killers are non-selective, and they will kill any plant they touch, so make sure none of it gets on your plants.

You can make an organic herbicide at home using vinegar, salt, and dish soap. To make it, mix 1 gallon (3.8L) of vinegar, 1 cup of salt, and 1 tablespoon of dish soap. The acidity in the vinegar destroys the cells of plants, the salt attacks the tissue, and the soap helps this mixture to stick to the plant. Like all organic herbicides, it is non-selective, which means it will kill all plants, not just weeds. It can also damage lawn grass. So, be careful when spraying it, and make sure it only gets on weeds.

To control weeds around the greenhouse, you can mow the area around it if necessary and then use herbicides. Before spraying weeds around the greenhouse with any herbicide, close the vents and windows to prevent spray drift from getting into the greenhouse. Before mowing or using an herbicide around the greenhouse, it's a good idea to use an insecticide, such as insecticidal soap, on the weeds to kill insects and prevent them from leaving the weeds and entering the greenhouse through vents.

Fertilizing

Synthetic fertilizers contain chemicals that have salts in them. These salts do not feed earthworms and other microorganisms in the soil. With time, the soil becomes acidic and loses important organisms that are needed to keep it healthy and fertile. The soil structure disintegrates, and the soil can no longer retain water. If the soil doesn't retain water and doesn't have the organisms it needs, your plants won't thrive.

Using organic fertilizers prevents this from happening. Organic fertilizers keep your soil healthy, and they're safe for you, your family, your pets, and the environment, whereas synthetic fertilizers are dangerous and can pollute the environment. Organic fertilizers are slower acting than chemical fertilizers, but organic ones are much better. Some synthetic fertilizers can burn plants because they're so harsh. Organic fertilizers are much gentler and safer. Organic fertilizers will improve your soil quality and increase good fungi and bacteria that the soil needs, whereas chemical fertilizers deplete this over time.

The key thing as an organic gardener is caring for the health of your soil. The soil needs to contain nutrients to create healthy, tasty plants. You can feed your soil with organic fertilizers. You can also make organic fertilizers at home. It is not expensive and not difficult at all. The most important nutrients plants need to grow are nitrogen (N), phosphorus (P), and potassium (K). Nitrogen is essential for photosynthesis and amino acid production. Phosphorus is required for growth and other functions, including photosynthesis and energy transfer. Potassium is used for root growth and photosynthesis.

When you have a no-dig garden, having organic matter and compost will improve your soil and its nutrient content, but you will also need additional organic fertilizers, such as wood ash, rock phosphate, animal byproducts, and manures (especially from animals that do not eat meat). Cow, goat, pig, and chicken droppings make great manure.

You can purchase organic fertilizers from garden centers. Organic fertilizers can be animal based (like bone meal, blood meal, fish meal, or fish emulsion), plant based (like cottonseed, alfalfa, or soybean meal, or seaweed), and there are also mineral fertilizers (like greensand or rock phosphate).

Usually on fertilizers you will see numbers shown on the side to indicate how much of each of the nutrients is in there. You may see numbers like 5-5-5 or 4-3-3. These numbers refer to N-P-K ratio, and they show how much of each of the nutrients (nitrogen, phosphorus, and potassium) the fertilizer contains. Fertilizers that have equal amounts of each of the nutrients are called balanced fertilizers, and they may have formulas like 5-5-5. For example, a fertilizer with a formula of 5-5-5 is a balanced fertilizer that has 5% nitrogen, 5% phosphorus, and 5% potassium. Balanced fertilizers work well for most plants, but for plants such as tomatoes and peppers and other fruiting plants, you can use a fertilizer with a higher K number. You can find which fertilizers are best for specific types of plants in individual plant profiles in Chapter 9.

If you buy an organic fertilizer from a garden center, simply follow the instructions on the label. Typically, you can use organic fertilizers every 2–4 weeks during the growing season on most vegetables.

Types of Fertilizers

There are many different types of fertilizers that you can use:

Dry fertilizers: These are typically added to garden beds or raised beds before planting, but they can also be used during the growing season. You would typically spread dry fertilizers 6 inches (15 cm) away from the base of your plants and water them thoroughly so that the nutrients can soak into the soil.

Liquid fertilizers: These are easily absorbed by the roots of plants, much quicker than dry fertilizers. They are usually used during the growing season to give your plants a boost of nutrients. They are perfect for growing vegetables, and they will help vegetables that grow quickly take up the nutrients they require. Liquid fertilizers are also perfect for fruiting or flowering plants, such as tomatoes, cucumbers, roses, and more.

Growth enhancers: These help your plants absorb nutrients effectively. A good example of this is kelp (a seaweed).

Homemade Organic Fertilizers

While you can purchase organic fertilizers from garden centers, you can also make them at home using a variety of different things. If you have a compost pile, you can make compost tea, which is essentially an organic liquid fertilizer for your plants (making compost will be covered in the next section of this chapter). Here's what you'll need to make compost tea:

- 3 to 4 gallons (11.4–15.2L) non-chlorinated water
- 2 to 6 cups compost
- 5-gallon (19L) bucket
- Shovel
- Strainer

Grab some compost from your compost pile with a shovel, and scoop up between 2 and 6 cups of compost. Add that to your empty bucket.

Next, you'll need some non-chlorinated water because chlorine will kill the good bacteria in your compost. You can use rainwater, or you can use tap water that has sat out for at least a day to allow the chlorine to evaporate. Add about 4 gallons (15.2L) of water to the compost in your bucket. Now you need to mix it all together. Make sure all of the compost gets completely submerged in water, and stir the mixture thoroughly so that the compost and water are combined.

Now you just need to leave the bucket in a place that's not in direct sunlight and let it sit so that the compost tea can brew. Don't leave the bucket in the sun because the heat can encourage the growth of harmful bacteria. Cold weather, rain, and snow can cause the tea to take longer to brew and can also kill beneficial microbes.

The amount of time your tea will take to brew depends on the air temperature outside. If it's above 60°F (15°C), let it sit for 12–36 hours. The lower the temperature, the longer it will take to brew. If the temperature is below 60°F (15°C), you may need to leave it for up to 72 hours. Stir the mixture once or twice a day while it's brewing.

Once the tea has finished brewing, you'll need to strain the compost from the liquid. If your compost tea isn't very dark, you don't need to dilute it. But if it's dark brown or black, you should dilute it with water to a ratio of 1:3 because it may be too strong for your plants. If you think your compost tea is not having the desired effect, you can dilute it less or even use it straight. If it's still too weak, you may need to brew the next batch longer. You can also try adding more compost to the mixture. Compost tea lasts about a week, so you'll need to use it quickly. You can use it every 2–4 weeks during the growing season as a liquid fertilizer.

Coffee grounds are a great source of nitrogen, and you can sprinkle these directly around your plants or make a liquid mix. Simply mix 2 cups of used coffee grounds with 5 gallons (19L) of water, and steep this mixture 3–4 days before using. You can use coffee grounds every 2–4 weeks during the growing season as a liquid fertilizer. Coffee grounds work especially well for nitrogen-loving plants, such as tomatoes, peppers, pole beans, blueberries, roses, and more.

You can also make Epsom salt fertilizer by dissolving 2 tablespoons of Epsom salt per gallon (3.8L) of water. Shake the mixture vigorously, and simply substitute this solution for normal watering once a month. It works because Epsom salt is made up of magnesium and sulfate, both of which are vital plant nutrients. It works especially well for magnesium-loving plants, such as tomatoes, peppers, potatoes, and roses.

Banana peels are very rich in potassium, and you don't even have to compost them. You can simply place these on your soil.

Another amazing organic fertilizer is seaweed. If you live near a beach, you can probably just collect some from there. If you collect fresh seaweed, you can dry it, then grind it, and sprinkle it around your plants.

Some weeds in your garden are full of nutrients, such as chickweed, burdock, and comfrey. You can fill a bucket ⅔ full of grass clippings and weeds and put in 2–3 inches (5–7.5 cm) of water, then let it sit for 3 days, stirring the mixture at least once a day. Keep it covered so that mosquitoes don't settle in it. Then you can spray this over plants, and it will help them grow.

If you keep chickens, goats, cows, or horses on your property, you can use their manure as organic fertilizer. You will need to compost it for best results.

Compost

Compost is decomposed organic matter that can be used as fertilizer to grow plants and to improve soil structure and texture. Three key things that are crucial for compost are nitrogen, carbon, and water. Compost is often called "black gold" because it is so valuable to the health of your soil and your plants. It is also versatile, as it has multiple uses in the garden. You can add compost to your garden when making new garden beds using the no-dig method. You can add it to raised beds when filling them, and you can also use it as mulch.

It is easy enough to make compost yourself from leaves and grass trimmings from your garden, any paper or cardboard from your house, and things like food scraps, vegetables that haven't been used, eggshells, tea bags, coffee grounds, fruit scraps, and so on.

You can purchase a compost bin or build a compost pile. This choice will depend on how much space you have and how much compost you need. If you have a small garden and not a lot of space, you should get a compost bin. Modern composters are streamlined and odor-free, and there are even small bins that you can keep in your kitchen. Or if you have the space, you can get larger outdoor versions, which are essentially a barrel with a crank that makes it easy to keep the contents mixed. If you need a lot of compost and have some free space in your garden, you can build a compost pile with wooden pallets or spare wood where you can store nitrogen items and carbon items separately, and then an area where these are layered together.

To make compost, you need to mix "green" materials (nitrogen), "brown" materials (carbon), and moisture. Green materials include kitchen scraps, like fruit and vegetable peels or waste, eggshells, coffee grounds as well as plants and grass trimmings. Brown materials include fallen leaves, tree branches, cardboard, newspapers, hay, straw, and wood shavings. You should have equal parts of green and brown materials. I would suggest alternating layers of green and brown materials. The final ingredient is moisture. Simply spray water on your compost to moisten it, but don't make it soggy. If it's too wet, it won't decompose properly.

There are things that you shouldn't add to compost, and this is because they will rot and smell bad and may attract rodents or larger wildlife. Do not add the following to your compost: meat, fish, dairy, fats, oils, any preserved wood, any diseased plants as well as any invasive weeds (as these could be passed onto your plants via the compost and keep spreading and growing). Don't add charcoal ash to compost because this could kill good bacteria, and definitely don't add dog or cat waste because it could contain harmful bacteria or parasites, and you don't want that in the soil that your plants are growing in.

Compost should heat up in order to decompose at a good rate. You can start your compost pile at any point throughout the year, but it will decompose quicker in the summer than in the winter.

To keep the decomposition rate on track, you'll need to take the temperature of your compost using a compost thermometer deep enough to get about $\frac{2}{3}$ of the way down. You can buy these online or at some garden centers. Make sure to take the temperature in several spots. The ideal temperature is between 130 and 140°F (55–60°C). If it gets up to 160°F (71°C) or more, you need to turn the pile with a pitchfork to aerate it, which will help bring the temperature down. If the temperature gets to 170°F (76°C) or above for more than several hours, this will stop microbes from working and kill the decomposing process. Try to keep the average temperature of your compost around 135°F (57°C).

If the compost starts to smell unpleasant, it could be that you have too much nitrogen (green materials), and you need to balance it with some brown materials. A properly balanced compost pile should not have any unpleasant smells. In fact, it should have a pleasant, earthy smell. If your compost starts to dry out, water it. You should it keep it moist but not soggy. You would typically need to water your compost once or twice a week. You should turn your compost every 2–4 weeks with a pitchfork. Once the compost starts to cool down and look like a black, crumbly material, then it's ready to use in the garden.

You can add compost in layers to create no-dig garden beds as mentioned previously. You can also add compost to raised beds when filling them. You can mix up to 30% of compost to the soil in raised beds. When you add compost to your garden beds or raised beds, it can reduce the need for fertilizers. You can also use it as mulch in your garden as well as raised beds. It will help keep your soil and plants' roots cool in the summer and warm in the winter, retain moisture, and prevent weeds from growing.

General Garden Care and Maintenance

If you want your plants to thrive throughout the growing season, you will need to schedule in some time to maintain your garden. As mentioned previously, one of the key tasks is watering, and this is essential to the health of your plants. Watering regularly will prevent plants from being stressed, and when plants are stressed, they're more prone to diseases and pests. If you don't water your plants regularly, you won't get a great harvest.

Apart from watering your plants, there are a few things you need to keep on top of, such as pruning your plants, removing dead/straggly plants and composting them, and providing support for plants that need it, all of which will be covered below.

Plant Growth Stages

Perhaps one of the most useful things I've learned about plants over the years is how to observe the stages of plant growth. All plants follow the same basic pattern of growth on their way to maturity, and knowing at which growth stage your plants are can help you know their needs better. Plants go through the following stages during their life cycle:

- Sprout
- Seedling
- Vegetative
- Budding
- Flowering
- Ripening

Plants start their life cycle as seeds. Depending on the type of plant, seeds can take anywhere between a few days to a few weeks to germinate and sprout. Seeds need air, water, and warmth to germinate and grow into seedlings.

As roots develop, sprouts grow into seedlings. They start growing true leaves, which look like baby versions of mature leaves. The main thing that seedlings need to grow is lots of light. If you grow seedlings indoors and they become leggy because they are not getting enough sunlight, you can get grow lights to provide more light to them. This will help them grow stronger and will help prevent legginess. Seedlings also need to be watered regularly because they can't store water for very long, so you'll need to keep the soil moist. They can also benefit from fertilizing. You can fertilize seedlings when they are at least 3 inches (7.5 cm) tall with a mild dose of liquid balanced fertilizer.

When seedlings move into the vegetative stage of their life cycle, plants focus on developing sturdy stems and green, leafy growth. From this point, plants need light, water, air, nutrients, and the right temperature to grow. You'll need to water your plants regularly and fertilize them to provide them with the nutrients they need. Regarding the right temperature, plants are divided into cool-season and warm-season crops. This will be covered in detail in plant profiles in Chapter 9. When plants are in the vegetative stage, they need nitrogen, which provides the nutrients that energize the building of new cells. You can use a balanced fertilizer at all growth stages for most plants with good results. However, you may consider using a fertilizer with a higher first number (nitrogen) during the vegetative stage.

As plants grow, they transition from the vegetative stage to the budding stage when they start shifting away from green growth toward producing buds, flowers, and then fruit. In this stage, plants need more phosphorus to help encourage budding. You might consider using a fertilizer with a higher second number (phosphorus) when plants are in the budding stage.

The next stage is flowering, and this is when buds become flowers and fruiting plants begin forming fruit where flowers grew. In this stage, nitrogen becomes less important, and plants need more potassium. Potassium is important for flowering, fruit production,

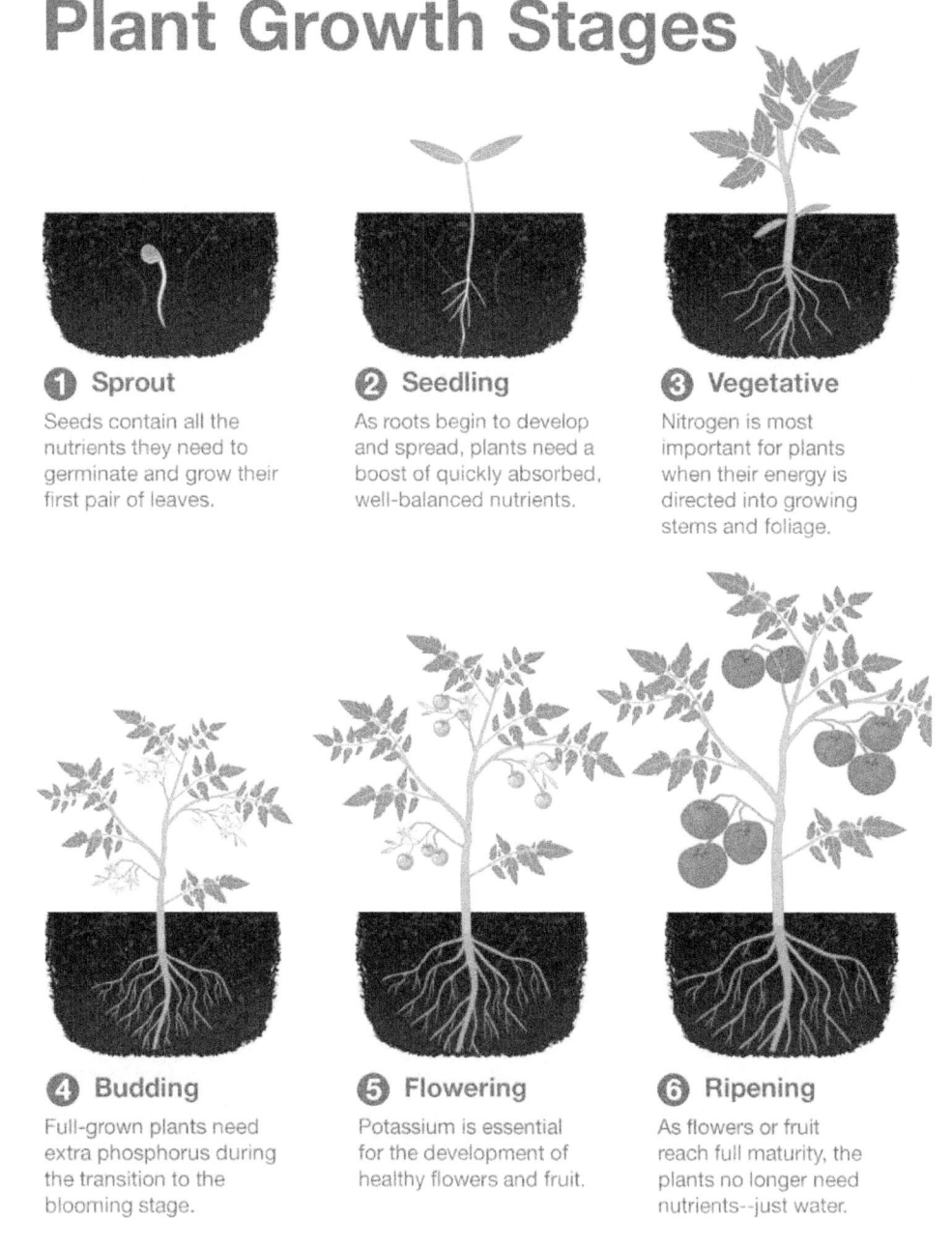

Plant Growth Stages

1 Sprout
Seeds contain all the nutrients they need to germinate and grow their first pair of leaves.

2 Seedling
As roots begin to develop and spread, plants need a boost of quickly absorbed, well-balanced nutrients.

3 Vegetative
Nitrogen is most important for plants when their energy is directed into growing stems and foliage.

4 Budding
Full-grown plants need extra phosphorus during the transition to the blooming stage.

5 Flowering
Potassium is essential for the development of healthy flowers and fruit.

6 Ripening
As flowers or fruit reach full maturity, the plants no longer need nutrients--just water.

and overall plant health. You may consider using a fertilizer with a higher third number (potassium) when plants are in the flowering stage.

The final stage is ripening, and this is when flowers and fruit ripen and mature. In this stage, plants no longer need added nitrogen for leafy growth because they focus their energy on finishing flowers and fruit. I would recommend that you stop fertilizing your plants in the ripening stage because when flowers and fruit are verging on full maturity, they need a week or two of just water without nutrients so that they can use up all the nutrients they have already absorbed. This process is known as flushing.

Deadheading, Pinching, and Pruning Plants

Deadheading means getting rid of a dead flower head of a plant. When flowers look brown and shriveled or have gone floppy and brown, you can pull these flowers off, or pinch the head off, or some will require you to cut the stem with pruners. When you deadhead plants, they will grow fuller and produce more flowers too. They will also continue to bloom for longer because they won't be wasting energy sending it to dead parts. Also, when you deadhead plants, you get rid of dead parts that are taking up space, so more oxygen can circulate around the plants, and more sunlight can get to the leaves when these are removed.

Pinching means removing the end of a plant just above a node on the stem where the leaves are attached. When pinching a plant, you remove the end set of leaves or buds, and in response, the plant sends out two new branches (also known as lateral stems), which results in more leaves and flowers. Pinching encourages branching on plants. It works especially well with herbs because it allows them to produce more desirable stems and leaves. It can also help keep plants compact. By pinching stems, you force the plant to focus on regrowing lost stems rather than growing tall. You can pinch your plants once they have formed a few pairs of leaves on the stem. You don't need to pinch your plants often—most plants can benefit from one or two pinching sessions during the growing season.

Pruning is removing parts of plants, trees, or vines that are not essential to growth or production and are no longer visually pleasing. If you prune any dead, damaged, or diseased bits of plants, this will help them to be healthy. When you're pruning a shrub, it's advisable to use varying lengths when cutting to make it look more natural, and you should be cutting branches just above buds or where a branch unites with another.

It's worth checking the guidelines for plants because some plants prefer to be pruned in late winter or early spring, whereas others should be pruned after they have bloomed in the spring. When you go to prune your plants, don't prune them in the hottest part of the day. If you're pruning deciduous plants (plants drop their leaves at the end of every growing season), early spring is a good time for this because the cuts will have plenty of time to heal before winter.

If your plants have grown really well but your garden beds or raised beds are overcrowded and the plants don't have room to grow, then pruning the plants can help.

Herbs should be given a regular trim. Some herbs will grow flowers, such as basil and cilantro (coriander). When they grow flowers, this changes the leaves and how the herb tastes. It can make herbs taste bitter, so herbs are typically harvested before they flower. A really good tip is that if you trim your herbs but don't intend to use them immediately and don't want them to go to waste, you could consider either drying them or putting them into ice cubes to use when you need them. Mint can look nice when its flowering, so you could leave a bit of this to give some nice aesthetic appearance to your garden and also attract pollinators, such as bumblebees, moths, and butterflies.

Support

As part of maintenance, you need to ensure that plants that require supports have them. There are trellises for cucumbers, raspberries, and blackberries. You can get bean wigwams, pea sticks, and obelisks for climbing plants and flowers. You can also get supporting hammocks for pumpkins, melons, watermelons, and other heavy vegetables and fruits.

Vegetables need sturdier trellises than vining flowers because they have heavy fruit. You can buy A-frame trellises—they are quite sturdy and durable. Another option is tomato cages, which are good for tomatoes, peppers, and bush squash. They can also be used for pole beans, cucumbers, and grapes. Vining plants will usually climb and wrap themselves around trellises of their own accord.

You can stake tall plants so that the wind doesn't blow them over and snap them. This works well for many vegetables, including tomatoes, eggplants, beans, peas, and more. It's best to place a stake when a plant is still young so that it can climb up the stake. You can put stakes in at the same time you are planting your plants, and you can stake plants in raised beds too.

You can buy stakes made of bamboo or vinyl-coated metal in most garden centers. Push the stake into the soil beside the plant. Make sure it's not taller than the plant itself. Once you've placed the stake, you'll need to tie your plant to the stake about ⅔ of the way up the stem, but be careful not to tie it too tight. This can damage your plant as it grows because the tie can cut into the plant's stem. Use stretchy ties to prevent this, such as special plant ties or strips of nylon. You can also use plant clips—they're easier to use than garden ties. Taller plants may need several ties at different points along the stems.

Pollination

The majority of vegetable plants don't need insect pollinators to produce fruit. They can be self-pollinating (tomatoes, eggplants, peppers, beans, peas), or they can use the wind to pollinate their flowers (strawberries, corn), or they are not grown for their flowers (carrots, potatoes, onions, garlic, lettuce, broccoli, cauliflower, and herbs). Plants that need insect pollinators include cucumbers, squash, pumpkins, watermelons as well as berry bushes and fruit trees.

In nature, plants can get pollinated via wind or insects and birds. In a greenhouse, you typically wouldn't get many bees or much wind, so you might need to either attract some bees or hand pollinate your plants. You can plant some flowers in and around your greenhouse to attract bees. Bees prefer blue-, yellow-, white-, and purple-colored flowers. Some flowers, like marigolds, also help deter pests while attracting pollinators.

Like all living creatures, bees need water. You can leave small containers with water around your garden to help attract pollinators. If you grow herbs, you can allow them to flower. Bees will swarm your garden if you do this. Letting herbs flower often makes their flavor weaker, but you don't have to let all your herbs flower. Leave a plant or two to flower—this will be more than enough. Bees love basil, mint, oregano, dill, fennel, and rosemary flowers.

Alternatively, you can pollinate your plants by hand. How a plant is pollinated depends on the type of flowers they have. Self-pollinating plants have perfect or complete flowers in which both male (stamen) and female (pistil) reproductive organs are contained in the same flower. Plants with imperfect flowers have male and female flowers growing separately. Hand pollination helps transports the pollen from male flowers to female flowers when there aren't enough pollinators around.

If you need to pollinate your plants by hand, it's best to do this in the morning hours when the humidity is high, which helps activate the pollen. Self-pollinating plants typically don't need hand pollination. Just a little bit of air movement or vibration is usually sufficient. Although these plants don't usually need hand pollination, you can help them along by gently tapping the flowers or using a small brush or a cotton swab to move the pollen from the stamen to the pistil. With strawberries, hand pollination can help improve yield. You can either transfer the pollen from the stamens on the outside of the flower to the pistils in the center with your finger, or a cotton swab, or a small, fine brush.

To pollinate plants with imperfect flowers, you'll need to identify male and female flowers first and then transfer the pollen from a male to a female flower using a cotton swab or a small, fine brush. Different plants have different flowers, so I'd recommend doing some research online to see how male and female flowers look on your plants. For example, cucumber male flowers often grow in clusters, and female flowers grow singly. Male flowers usually appear first on cucumber plants, and female flowers begin at a small fruit, which makes them easier to identify. Squash male flowers have a plain stem below the flower, and female flowers have a tiny rudimentary squash below the petals.

To pollinate plants with imperfect flowers, gently peel back a petal from a male flower to uncover the male anther that carries the pollen. Use a cotton swab or a small, fine brush to pick up the pollen and apply it onto the stigma of a female flower of the same plant. You can use the same male flower to pollinate several female flowers.

Anther

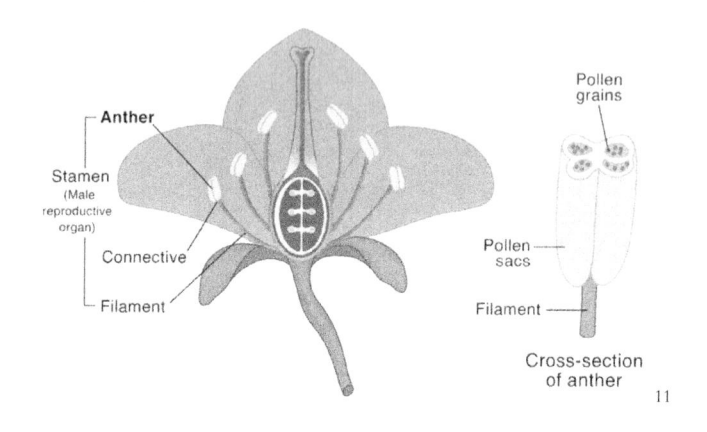

[11]

---

[11] Image from https://www.sciencefacts.net/anther.html

Stigma

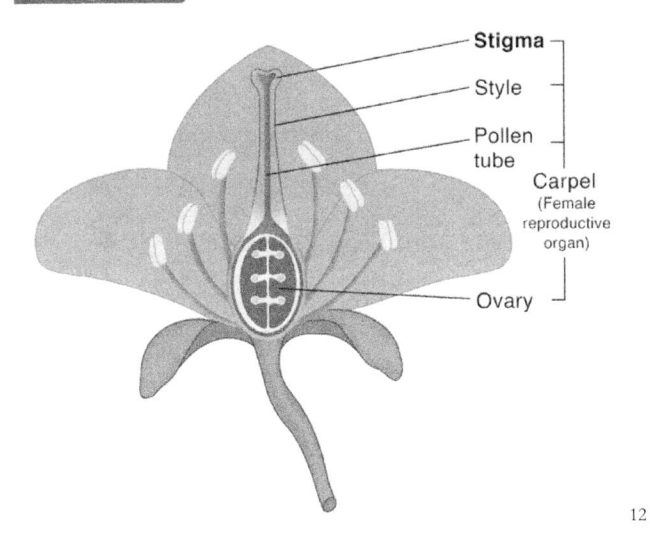

[Diagram of flower showing: Stigma, Style, Pollen tube, Carpel (Female reproductive organ), Ovary]

12

General Welfare

As mentioned previously, you will need to water and fertilize your plants regularly. You will also want to ensure that all your plants look the best they are able to by pruning and deadheading plants to get rid of dead flowers and dead or overgrown stems or branches. If plants have grown too tall (leggy) and aren't blooming, you'll need to cut them down. You'll have to take out any plants that are dead or not doing well and replace them with new plants. Most importantly, you'll need to check your plants for pests and any signs of diseases regularly. Dealing with pests and diseases will be covered in the next chapter.

Greenhouse Maintenance and Cleaning

Whether made from glass, polycarbonate, or polyethylene plastic, all greenhouses can benefit from periodic cleaning and maintenance. A routine or annual cleaning is essential to prevent unwanted pests and diseases from moving in and keep your greenhouse in tip-top shape. While greenhouses provide a wonderful growing environment for plants, they also provide the perfect conditions for pests to overwinter. Insects and pests can get into cracks and crevices and hibernate there.

Just as in your home, much of the maintenance for your greenhouse involves cleaning. If you have a year-round greenhouse, you would need to clean it regularly (I clean mine seasonally, usually every 3 months or so), but if it's only seasonal, then a fall clean up at the end of the growing season is usually enough. With that said, let's take a look at maintaining and cleaning your greenhouse step-by-step.

First of all, clean up any fallen leaves, debris, and plant matter, including any weeds that are trying to get a foothold on earthen floors. While they will decompose and enrich the soil, they also attract pests, so it's best to gather any fallen leave and debris and add them to your compost pile (only if there are no pests on them). Also, take note of any existing diseases or pests, and remove any leaves and/or plant parts that are heavily infested. Do not add them to your compost pile, but bag them up and dispose of them in the trash.

Next, you can wash all greenhouse tools and accessories, including gardening tools, pots, trays, and other equipment. Wash everything thoroughly using soapy water and let sit in an oxygen bleach solution of ¾ cup oxygen bleach to 1 gallon (3.8L) of water.

Dealing with pests and diseases will be covered in detail in the next chapter; however, throughout the growing season, you should remove parts of plants that develop diseases (or whole plants if they can't be saved) or become heavily infested with pests as soon as you notice them. This will not only limit the spread

---

[12] Image from https://www.sciencefacts.net/stigma.html

but will also make cleaning up easier. Also, make sure to keep on top weeding both inside and around your greenhouse, as weeds can host pests and diseases.

The frame of a greenhouse provides a great hiding place for overwintering pests. Metal frame greenhouses aren't as susceptible to this but still need disinfecting. Wood is the worst in this regard, as it provides cracks and crevices that pests can use as a hideout. To prevent pests from infesting your greenhouse frame, you can wash your entire greenhouse structure and glass down using an oxygen bleach solution. You need to wash it all, so you'll likely need a step ladder to get to the roof.

If you have a wooden frame or foundation, you can use caulk to seal any cracks or holes, and this will help prevent heat loss through these cracks and will also prevent pests from hiding in them. You can also apply a vegetable-based horticultural oil onto all exposed wood (most horticultural oils are organic and won't damage your plants). This is best done using a brush to ensure the oil reaches into all the cracks to suffocate hiding pests.

If you have an irrigation system, then disinfecting it can be a good idea. Irrigation lines and holding tanks develop algae and can host pests, such as gnats. Use ¾ cup oxygen bleach to 1 gallon (3.8L) of hot water to make a cleaning solution, and use it to flush lines, soak any dripper heads, and scrub out holding tanks.

Finally, if you have a heater, fans, or other heating or cooling devices, make sure to check them regularly. This way, you can detect small problems before they become big ones. Perform any scheduled maintenance recommended by the manufacturer, such as lubricating, cleaning, and so on.

Maintaining my garden and my greenhouses is second nature to me, and it is a part of my daily morning routine and a part of the day that I really look forward to. I water the vegetables if they require it, and I pull up any weeds as I go. I check the health of the plants and ensure there are no signs of pests or diseases. I check that plants are correctly supported and encourage climbing plants with the trellises I have for them. After I've watered the plants, I take a basket and harvest any vegetables or fruits that are ready. I have them in a plastic basket that I can hose to wash off any debris before taking the produce I've harvested into the house. As for greenhouse maintenance, I clean my year-round greenhouse seasonally, usually every 3 months or so, and my seasonal greenhouses at the end of the growing season. I also check for any structural damage as well as all the electrical devices and accessories, such as fans, heaters, and so on, regularly and make any repairs as needed.

Key takeaways from this chapter:

1. To maintain your garden, water it, remove weeds, mulch your garden beds and raised beds, check plant health, check your plants for any signs of pests or diseases, and ensure that plants that need supports have them.
2. You can use things like outside taps, water butts, a hose reel, or you can hook up a hose to a well to help water your garden.
3. Many variables affect how much water your vegetable garden needs, such as soil, climate, weather, the type of plants you're growing, and more.
4. Stick your finger 1 inch (2.5 cm) deep into the soil to feel the moisture. If it is dry, water it. If it feels moist, wait.

5. Too little or too much water can be damaging for plants. Check for signs if your plants are underwatered or overwatered.
6. It is best to water plants in the morning. Water your plants at the base, and don't splash the leaves.
7. If you have raised beds, drip line irrigation is ideal. You can have it on a timer, which is really convenient.
8. You should mulch your garden beds and raised beds to prevent weeds and keep the moisture in. Keep on top of weeding so that it is quick maintenance and not an onerous chore.
9. Organic fertilizers are better than synthetic ones because synthetic fertilizers contain salts, which make the soil acidic and make it deteriorate quickly. Organic fertilizers are slower acting, but they are much better and safer for you, your soil, and your plants. You can make organic fertilizers out of compost, coffee beans, and seaweed. You can also use banana peels as fertilizer.
10. You can make compost out of kitchen scraps, leaves, grass trimmings, paper, cardboard, and so on. Turn your compost periodically to add air, and water it gently to give it some moisture.
11. Deadhead, pinch, and prune plants so that they bloom for longer. Check pruning guidelines for when to prune plants, and don't prune at the hottest part of the day. Prune back herbs—this will help make them taste less bitter after flowering.
12. Support climbing plants with trellises, canes, wigwams, obelisks, poles, and so on. This applies to peas, beans, raspberries, cucumbers, and other plants.
13. Check your plants for any signs of pests or diseases.
14. Just as in your home, much of the maintenance for your greenhouse involves cleaning. If you have a year-round greenhouse, you would need to clean it regularly (I clean mine seasonally, usually every 3 months or so), but if it's only seasonal, then a fall clean up at the end of the growing season is usually enough.
15. If you have a wooden frame or foundation, you can use caulk to seal any cracks or holes. You can also apply a vegetable-based horticultural oil onto all exposed wood, which will kill pests that hide in the cracks.
16. Make sure to check your accessories and devices, such as drip irrigations systems, heaters, fans, and so on, regularly, and perform maintenance suggested by the manufacturer.

The next chapter will look at pest control and dealing with diseases. It will discuss various organic options to deal with pests rather than using chemical pesticides. The chapter will also look at dealing with diseases and using companion planting and crop rotation for pest control and disease prevention.

Chapter 7: Pest Control and Dealing with Diseases

Once you have established a wonderful vegetable garden, you want to be able to see it grow, develop, and come to fruition, and you deserve to reap the harvest of lovely, fresh vegetables filled with vitamins to help you live a healthy, sustainable lifestyle. So, naturally, the last thing you want is your crop getting eaten and damaged by pests and diseases.

To prevent your vegetables from getting damaged by pests or them becoming diseased, you need to inspect your plants each week. If you have spaced your plants with plenty of room between them, this will make them less prone to fungal diseases, like powdery mildew.

This chapter will cover how you can spot common garden pests. It will discuss a wide variety of organic pest control options so that you can maintain a sustainable garden. It will give you information about attracting beneficial insects to your garden to assist with pest and disease control. Also, common garden diseases will be covered as well as disease prevention. This chapter will also cover how crop rotation and companion planting can help prevent diseases and specific companion plants for disease management.

Common Garden Pests

Pests can damage your plants in a variety of ways. Some will target the roots, some may chew up the leaves, some pests feed on other pests, and some will spread diseases through plants in your garden. This section will cover some common types of pests you should look out for, and the next section will cover how you can deal with them using organic options.

Aphids

Aphids are a common garden pest. They are small, 1/16- to 1/8-inch-long (2–4 mm), pear-shaped, soft-bodied insects. They can be a variety of different colors, including green, black, red, yellow, brown, or gray. They attack a lot of different plants, including tomatoes, lettuce, kale, and cabbage, and they especially love flowering plants. They suck the sap out of stems and new leaves.

[13]

If your plants ever look yellow or brown or if they curl or wilt, do check to ensure there are no aphids on your plants. Because aphids leave behind honeydew (a

---
[13] Image from http://www.balconycontainergardening.com/wildlife/633-tips-for-aphid-control

sugary liquid that is released as they eat your plants), this can cause sooty mold on your plants. If your garden also has ants, this will exacerbate the aphid issue because ants and aphids work hand in hand. Ants will protect aphids because ants like honeydew. A great biological control to deal with aphids is to stop ants first, and this will be discussed in the next section of this chapter that covers dealing with pests.

Ants

Having some ants in the garden is nothing to worry about, but if there are lots of them, they might become a problem. If you have other pests, such as aphids, soft scales, mealybugs, and whiteflies, ants love them because all these pests produce honeydew, which is one of their favorite things to eat. Ants often protect these pests from predators and parasites so that they can continue to produce honeydew. Dealing with ants can help reduce the abundance of honeydew-producing pests.[14]

Cabbage Worms

These are green caterpillars that turn into yellow-white butterflies sometimes with up to 4 black spots on their wings. You will find these on cabbage, kale, cauliflower, broccoli, turnips, radishes, Brussels sprouts, and kohlrabi. They will chew holes in leaves and flowers.[15]

Carrot Rust Flies

Carrot rust flies are small, shiny, and black, and they have an orange head and legs. Their larvae look like tiny maggots. These can affect carrots, parsnips, celeriac, celery, and parsley. They will leave tunnels in your vegetables and scar them.

Caterpillars

Caterpillars can rampage over your garden, munching up leaves, stalks, and stems and making your plants look tatty and damaged. They often show

---

[14] Image from https://www.gardeningknowhow.com/plant-problems/pests/insects/ants-in-flower-pots.htm

[15] Image from https://kelloggarden.com/blog/gardening/how-to-get-rid-of-cabbage-worms/

up around late summer and early fall, and they can be a really annoying pest of fall vegetables, like cabbage, kale, collards, broccoli, and cauliflower.[16]

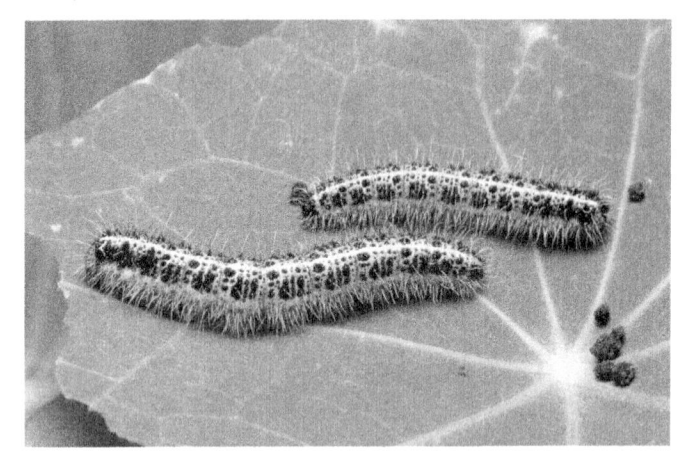

Colorado Potato Beetles

These beetles are about ⅜ of an inch (1 cm) long, with a bright yellow/orange body and 10 bold, brown stripes along the length of their bodies. They will eat tomatoes as well as potatoes and other garden crops, like peppers, tomatillos, and eggplants. They will strip the leaves of plants until they look like skeletons. They tend to eat the top of plants first.[17]

Cucumber Beetles

These beetles are yellow, have yellow wings, and they have 3 longitudinal black stripes. They'll go on melons, cucumbers, gourds, squash, and sometimes on corn, beans, beets, and other vegetables. They will make holes in leaves and can transmit bacterial wilt.[18]

Cutworms

These turn into brown or gray moths. In the caterpillar stage, they can be yellow, green, brown, or gray. They love to eat young seedlings, especially broccoli, tomatoes, cabbage, and kale.[19]

---

[16] Image from https://www.nature-and-garden.com/gardening/organic-treatment-caterpillars.html

[17] Image from https://uwm.edu/field-station/colorado-potato-beetle-redux/

[18] Image from https://extension.usu.edu/pests/research/cucumber-beetles

[19] Image from https://gardenerspath.com/how-to/disease-and-pests/control-cutworms/

Flea Beetles

These beetles jump like fleas. They damage young plants by leaving holes in the leaves, and their larvae eat plants' roots, which can destroy a plant completely. They can be found on radishes, potatoes, tomatoes, corn, and eggplants.[20]

Leaf Miners

You can often tell that your plants have leaf miners if you see trails on the leaves. The trails wind round and may look silver or beige. They appear on vegetables, shrubs, bushes, and perennials. These are caused by larvae of a small dark fly. A female fly will make little cuts in the leaf surface and lay her eggs there, and the larvae will tunnel inside the leaf just under the surface. They will feed there, and after 2–3 weeks they'll emerge as adults.

This mostly just makes the leaves of your plants look unpleasant, but if there's a lot of damage to leaves, then the plant could become weak and even die. One of the most effective ways to get rid of this is to remove infected leaves as soon as you see the trails and dispose of them. Don't add these leaves to compost. Bag them up and dispose of them in the trash.

Mealybugs

Mealybugs look like white, cottony masses that appear on the leaves, stems, and fruit of plants. They have a sucking mouthpart that draws sap out of plants. Plants will turn yellow, curl, and become weak. Mealybugs produce honeydew, which can encourage sooty mold to grow and attract ants. They attack a lot of different plants, including asparagus, beans, beets, cabbage, cucumbers, lettuce, peppers, pumpkins, tomatoes, and more.[21]

---

[20] Image from https://extension.usu.edu/vegetableguide/cucumber-melon-pumpkin-squash/flea-beetles

[21] Image from https://wallygrow.com/blogs/feature/how-to-get-rid-of-mealybug-on-houseplants

Mexican Bean Beetles

These are a common garden pest. These beetles are copper in color and have 16 black spots. Their larvae are yellow with bristly spines. They love all types of beans: green beans, pole beans, snap beans, runner beans, lima beans, and soybeans. They will eat leaves until they look like skeletons.[22]

Pill Bugs

Pill bugs aren't really going to harm your plants, so if you see some near your plants, you shouldn't worry too much about it. However, if you see masses of them, then you may need to do something about it. There are a number of ways to get rid of pill bugs, and one way is to ensure you have food for them that is away from your garden. For example, you could have a compost pile out of the way, and this should keep pill bugs happy and away from your plants.

Pill bugs love dark and damp conditions, so they often live under debris in the garden. Cleaning up the debris from leaves, grass clippings, pieces of wood, and so on can help reduce their population. A top tip is that you can put a toilet paper tube around seedlings, and this will stop pill bugs from reaching them.[23]

Root-Knot Nematodes

Nematodes are parasite worms that burrow into roots, and this stops the roots from absorbing the necessary water and nutrients. You can check the roots of your plants by pulling out one plant and looking at the roots to see if there are little balls or knots in the roots. To treat nematodes, once you have harvested the crop, you can bring the roots out into the sun, and direct sunlight will kill nematodes. You can also put French marigold plants near plants with nematodes because French marigold roots release a chemical that is toxic to nematodes.

Slugs and Snails

These will eat plants in your garden, especially low hanging plants in the shade or where it's damp. Slugs and snails can carry lungworm, which can be dangerous to pets. They will attack any young seedlings and

---

[22] Image from https://val.vtecostudies.org/projects/lady-beetle-atlas/mexican-bean-beetle/

[23] Image from https://www.thoughtco.com/fascinating-facts-about-pillbugs-4165294

a great variety of plants. They will leave holes in leaves. They eat at night and love rainy days. You won't see them often throughout the day.[24]

Spider Mites

Spider mites are very common. They're extremely small, and they have 8 legs and can be red, green, yellow, or brown. They emerge in the spring and eat plants, which makes the plants weak and susceptible to diseases. They attack a lot of different plants, but they're especially attracted to strawberries, tomatoes, melons, and fruit trees. A female spider mite can lay hundreds of eggs and infestations grow really quickly. Definitely look under the leaves of plants because they will hide there.

If the infestation is really bad, remove infested leaves and dispose of them in the trash. Don't add these infested leaves to your compost because the infestation could spread.

Springtails

Springtails love moisture, and they swarm together in clouds that you can see in the air. They can be brown, gray, black, or white. They like wet soil, rotting straw, decaying leaves, and other damp organic matter. They feed on mold, fungi, and algae. They are mostly a nuisance pest and won't damage plants or harm people or pets. They will chew roots in the soil where they're located, which can inhibit plant hardiness, but they rarely do significant damage. If the soil dries out, they will likely find a new home.[25]

Squash Bugs

Squash bugs feed on cucumbers, squash, melons, pumpkins, and zucchini. They suck juice from the leaves and stems of plants. Leaves damaged by squash bugs will be mottled with yellow, and they may go crispy and die.[26]

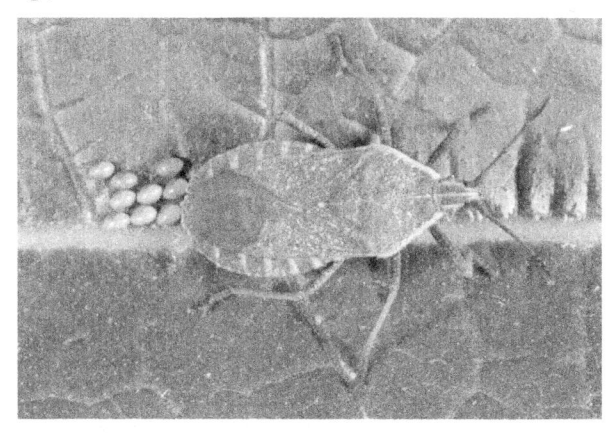

---

[24] Image from https://ucanr.edu/blogs/blogcore/postdetail.cfm?postnum=46093&

[25] Image from https://www.planetnatural.com/pest-problem-solver/houseplant-pests/springtail-control/

[26] Image from https://www.purdue.edu/hla/sites/yardandgarden/dont-let-sap-sucking-squash-bugs-get-old/

Thrips

Thrips are tiny insects—they are usually 2 millimeters in length. They attack a variety of different vegetables, including onions, beans, carrots, squash, and more. When they're young, they are pale yellow. When they're adults, they are brown or black. If the leaves of your plants are looking dull or have a silver mottling, you may have thrips. If you look really close at the leaves, you may see little black dots on them.

Certain plants tend to get thrips more often, and these include onions, peas, tomatoes, cucumbers, beans, carrots, and many flowers, especially gladioli and roses. Thrips like dry and hot conditions, so if you increase humidity around your plants, this can discourage them. If you get rid of dead leaves and fallen flowers off plants, this can discourage thrips too.[27]

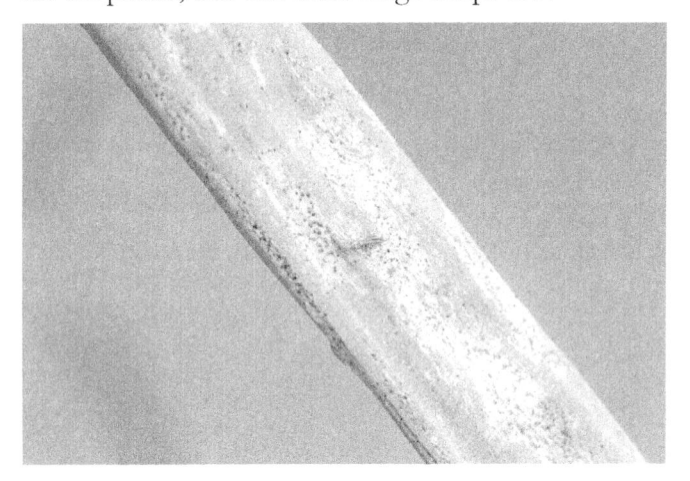

Tomato or Tobacco Hornworms

Hornworm caterpillars turn into brown or gray moths. They will attack tomatoes, potatoes, peppers, eggplants, and tobacco. They eat the leaves, usually the tops of plants, and leave dark pellets of excrement behind.

Vine Weevils

These beetles will eat the leaves of plants in the summer, and their larvae will attack the roots of plants, which can cause plants to die. Vine weevils attack a wide variety of plants, but they are especially attracted to flowers, like cyclamen, fuchsias, polyanthus, primulas, and also strawberries.[28]

Whiteflies

Whiteflies are sap-sucking pests, and they target vegetables, such as tomatoes, eggplants, peppers, okra,

---

[27] Image from https://www.gardenersworld.com/how-to/solve-problems/thrips/

[28] Image from https://luv2garden.com/identify-and-control-black-vine-weevils/

and brassicas, as well as ornamental plants. They produce honeydew, which can lead to sooty black mold and attract ants. Look for yellow leaves and white ovals under leaves which may be whitefly eggs.[29]

Organic Pest Control Methods

Using organic pesticides is less damaging to the soil and environment rather than using chemical pesticides. Organic methods of pest control do work and can even be more effective than chemical pesticides in some cases. It was mentioned in the introduction to this chapter, but it is super important to regularly check your plants for pest damage because the sooner you identify it, the sooner it can be dealt with. A few holes in plants is nothing to worry about, but if damage is getting out of hand, you may need to do something about it.

Organic Pesticides/Sprays

You can purchase organic pesticides from garden centers to help control pests. Make sure to check the packaging carefully to make sure the spray you're purchasing is organic. They will contain *Bacillus*, which is a bacterium. They may have neem oil and copper in them too. You can also make your own organic pesticides from household products or plants. It is advisable to spray both store bought and homemade pesticides on a small part of a plant rather than the whole thing at first just to check it doesn't damage it. Also, don't spray pesticides in really hot sun because this can burn plants.

You can make sprays for pest control at home. Here are some of my favorite recipes:

Neem Oil Spray

Neem oil is typically used when you have a pest infestation, but you can spray your plants with a neem oil solution every 2–3 weeks as a preventative measure. This is good to get rid of soft-bodied insects, such as aphids, fungus gnats, whiteflies, scales, squash bugs, Colorado potato beetles, and mealybugs. Neem oil also works well for treating leaf miners. Pests won't lay eggs after being sprayed, and they will eat less and grow more slowly. Neem oil spray would sadly work on beneficial insects too, so you could spray early in the morning or late in the afternoon, and then cover your plants with a row cover to stop them from being affected. It can also prevent powdery mildew. It does

---

[29] Image from https://www.naplesgarden.org/container-gardening-bugs-friends-or-foes/

have quite a strong smell. Simply follow the instructions on the label, make a spray, and spray your plants every 3–4 days until pests are gone.

Insecticidal Soap

You can buy insecticidal soap or make homemade insecticidal soap by mixing 1 tablespoon of liquid soap with a quart (0.95L) of water. Just like neem oil, insecticidal soap works well against soft-bodied insects. Simply follow the instructions on the label, make a spray, and use it to spray your plants once or twice a week until pests are gone.

Chili Pepper Spray

This spray is effective against most insects and pests attacking your plants. Mix half a cup of chopped hot peppers, 2 cups of water, and 2 tablespoons of dish soap (with no bleach). Let this mixture sit overnight, strain it, then put it in a spray bottle and spray on plants. Spray your plants every 3–4 days until the infestation is gone.

Garlic Spray

This is great for getting rid of pest and insect infestations. You can make this out of a head of garlic, a tablespoon of dish soap (with no bleach), 2 tablespoons of vegetable oil, and 2 cups of water. Mix the ingredients together, and allow the mixture to sit overnight. Then put it in a spray bottle and spray on plants. Garlic has fungicidal effects, and it's good for getting rid of aphids, squash bugs, whiteflies, and other pests. Spray your plants every 3–4 days until pests are gone.

Oil Spray

This solution is super easy to make. It works great against aphids, mealybugs, mites, leaf miners, whiteflies, and beetle larvae. Simply mix a tablespoon of vegetable oil, 2 tablespoons of baking soda, 1 teaspoon of dish soap, and 2 quarts (1.9 L) of water. Put the mixture into a spray bottle, and spray it on affected plants. Spray as necessary until pests are gone.

Soap Spray

This will help get rid of pests and insects and will keep your plants safe. Soap spray works well against aphids, whiteflies, mealybugs, thrips, spider mites, and other soft-bodied pests and insects. It doesn't work well against larger insects, such as caterpillars, sawflies, and beetle larvae, however. Simply mix 2 teaspoons of dish soap with a quart (0.95 L) of water. The insects become dehydrated and die when you spray them with this. You will need to spray your plants every 4–7 days until pests are gone.

Apart from sprays, there are other organic methods to deal with pests:

Water

You can spray your plants with a hose to remove pests like aphids, spider mites, and thrips, but don't blast your plants with water because this can damage them.

Remove Pests by Hand

You can pick off some pests by hand. This is easy to do this with snails, slugs, caterpillars, Colorado potato beetles, and squash bugs. Most insects won't harm you, but you can wear rubber gloves just in case. You will need to kill the insects or place them in a plastic bag or a container with a lid that they can't escape from. Keeping your garden clean also helps prevent pests. While fallen leaves and fruits will decompose and enrich the soil with nutrients, they can also attract pests. You can clear away any dropped or fallen leaves or fruits and add them to your compost pile if they are not diseased.

Nip Off Infected or Infested Parts of Plants

One of the best organic prevention and control methods for pests and diseases is to regularly inspect your plants and physically remove any pests or diseased areas. You can nip off infected or infested leaves or buds or pull up infected crops. You can prune off parts of plants that look like they have a disease or pests.

Diatomaceous Earth (DE)

You can use a shaker to pest-proof plants with this powder. This absorbs the moisture from the bodies of insects and pests. It will work against slugs, aphids, caterpillars, and thrips. It will, however, also kill beneficial insects, so be careful with it. You can put it on the soil around your plants. If you have any leaves that show signs of an infestation, then you can put it underneath the leaves.

Exclusion

To protect young seedlings from being attacked by cutworms, you can put a toilet paper tube around them and bury it ½ an inch (1.2 cm) into the ground. This works well to protect cabbage seedlings from cabbage root flies and cabbage maggot flies too.

Another exclusion technique is to put abrasive strips of materials on the soil around plants, which can help repel slugs, snails, and caterpillars. You could create barriers with sawdust, wood ashes, crushed eggshells, seashells, or coffee grounds, and all of these will break down and feed the soil with time too.

You can also set up copper or steel wires around your raised beds and have 2 wires close together connected to a 9V battery to create an electric fence for slugs and snails. While this may prevent any further snails getting in, the ones that are already there will continue to eat your plants. You could put copper around your garden beds too because copper has a chemical reaction with snail and slug slime, which repels them.

Mulch helps protects plants from soil splashing on their leaves, and it will also stop pests from laying eggs on the surface of the soil.

Dealing with Ants

If you spot a lot of ants in your garden, try to find ant trails and follow them to see where they lead you. Ant trails usually lead to ant mounds, where all the ants live alongside their queen ant. You need to kill the queen ant to destroy a colony. You can pour boiling water onto the mound, and it may reach the queen through the tunnels. However, it may sometimes not work because even boiling water cools down quickly on contact with earth, or the queen may be deeper underground, and water might not reach her.

Using borax is a much more effective way of dealing with ants. Mix ½ cup sugar, 1½ tablespoons of borax, and 1½ cups of water. Soak some cotton balls in the mixture, and put them in places where you see lots of ants. Sugar will attract the ants, and they will take borax to their home, where they will eat it later. Eating borax will kill the ants.

Attracting Beneficial Insects for Pest Control

It is far better to attract beneficial insects to your garden to sort out pests for you than it is to use pesticides. Chemical pesticides will get rid of beneficial insects as well as bad ones and can put chemicals on vegetables and fruits that you'll consume, plus they impact the environment—water, air, and wildlife. Even organic pesticides will affect beneficial insects, so it's best to spray them early in the morning or late in the afternoon to stop beneficial insects, such as bees and ladybugs, from being affected. If you create a good environment for beneficial insects, they will come to your garden and eat pests, which is cheaper and safer than using pesticides. Insects are becoming more resistant to chemical pesticides, but beneficial insects can get rid of them by eating them or laying eggs on them, which kills the host.

There are approximately 1 million insects that have been discovered and classified, and less than 1% of these are pests. So, a far greater number of insects in your garden either won't harm it or are actually beneficial to your garden. Beneficial insects are the ones that eat pests that would otherwise munch upon your delicious vegetables. These are known as predators and can include ladybugs, lacewings, and praying mantises. There are also beneficial parasitic insects. They lay their eggs on pests, and when the eggs hatch, the larvae eat the host. And there are also pollinators who pollinate flowers in the garden, and these include bees, moths, butterflies, and flies.

Ladybugs are good insects to have. They are natural predators to aphids, chinch bugs, asparagus beetle larvae, alfalfa weevils, bean thrips, grape root worms, Colorado potato beetles larvae, spider mites, whiteflies, and mealybugs, among other insects, which means they will eat them. You could grow flowers and herbs, such as cilantro (coriander), dill, fennel, caraway, yarrow, tansy, angelica, scented geraniums, coreopsis, and cosmos, in and around your greenhouse to attract them.

Lacewings are great to have in your garden. In their larval stage, they look like small ½-inch (1.2 cm) alligators, and they will happily eat aphids, caterpillars, mealybugs, leafhoppers, whiteflies, and insect eggs. You can plant cilantro (coriander), dill, yarrow, cosmos, and tansy to attract them. Hover flies are also great to have around. They may look like a small bee, but as they move through the air, they are more fly-like in their appearance. Planting dill, parsley, yarrow, caraway, and lavender will help attract them to your garden.

If you're unsure about which are good insects and which are bad, try to see whether the bugs are eating your garden or defending it by eating other insects. Look to see whether the bugs are chewing holes in your leaves or eating other bugs. You could use a folding 10x power hand lens to help you see the bugs better. If you see bugs in your garden, you can make a description of the bug and then do an Internet search on it or ask in gardening groups on Facebook or gardening forums. You need to find out if it's beneficial or harmful and attract more of the beneficial ones to your garden.

Beneficial nematodes will control soil dwelling pests. The most common ones are *Steinernema carpocapsae* and *Heterorhabditis bacteriophora*. These nematodes search for insects they can use as hosts, and they release bacteria that kill the hosts once inside. If you are suffering from carrot flies, you can release beneficial nematodes into the soil near your carrots, and they will eat the larvae. *Steinernema* is a good nematode to use. You can also use a microbial pest control agent called Bt (*Bacillus thuringiensis*). There are different types of Bt. For example, Btk (*Bacillus thuringiensis kurstaki*) is a subspecies of Bt that targets mosquitoes, fungus gnats, and black fly larvae as well as caterpillars, like cabbage worms, tomato hornworms, cabbage loopers, and gypsy moths. Bt var. san diego (*Bacillus thuringiensis var. san diego*) are used to get rid of Colorado potato beetles. Bt var. san diego has a manufacturing process that includes genetic engineering, however, so it's not approved by the National Organic Program (NOP). Bt and Btk are organic are certified for use in organic agriculture and gardening.

Dealing with Diseases

Diseases in plants are usually caused by fungi, bacteria, or viruses. If you have high humidity and warm temperatures, look for fungal and bacterial diseases. In the summer, look for viral diseases. Nematodes love warm weather but can impact the roots of plants all year round.

Because you'll be maintaining your garden on a daily basis, it's generally quite easy to spot if your plants are suffering from any diseases. You should try to tackle these swiftly before they become a big issue and spread.

If you buy plants from a nursery, check that they're healthy. Ensure your plants have enough water, sunlight, and enough space for air to flow around them. You can save plants from some diseases, especially if you catch them early on, but if your plants are beyond saving, you'll have to remove them and dispose of them in a plastic bag in the trash. Never put infected plants in a compost pile.

If you have been working with diseased plants, then ensure you wash your hands, tools, and gardening gloves before handling any other plants to avoid spreading diseases. If you don't live in a tropical area but are growing tropical plants, these may be more prone to diseases because they're not native to the area and haven't built up resistance to local garden pests.

Fungal Diseases

If you see that your plants are wilting, or you have noticed spots on your plants' leaves, or if you can see rotten plant stems, this could be due to a fungal disease. Fungi thrive in dark and damp conditions, so too much humidity can cause fungal diseases in plants. To prevent fungal diseases from occurring, water your plants at the base, and make sure that plenty of air can circulate around your plants and that all your plants get a good amount of sunlight.

Fungicides are used to treat fungal diseases, although not all diseases can be treated by fungicides. You can purchase organic fungicides, such as neem oil, horticultural oil, copper, sulfur, bicarbonates, and others, from garden centers. If you use copper fungicides for an extended period of time, copper levels can build up in the soil and kill earthworms and other beneficial organisms. Neem oil fungicides affect beneficial insects, so try to use them early in the morning or in the evening. You can also make homemade organic fungicides with baking soda or apple cider vinegar.

To make a fungicide with baking soda, mix 4 teaspoons of baking soda and 1 teaspoon of mild soap with a gallon (3.8L) of water. This fungicide recipe works especially well for stopping powdery mildew. Mix all the ingredients together, and put the mixture in a spray bottle. Spray all infected leaves top and bottom, and make sure to cover all the leaves with a thick layer of the mixture so that it drips off the leaves. It can be a good idea to spray the entire plant and not just infected leaves because fungus could be hiding where you can't see it.

To make a fungicide with apple cider vinegar, mix 4 tablespoons of apple cider vinegar with a gallon (3.8L) of water. This simple recipe has helped me save dozens, if not hundreds, of plants. Try to spray this mixture early in the day so that the sun and acid don't burn your plants. This also works well as a preventative spray. You can spray it every 2–3 weeks just in case.

You can also mix 1 quart (0.95L) of warm water, 1 teaspoon of mouthwash, and 1 tablespoon of hydrogen peroxide to make another good homemade fungicide. Mix all the ingredients together, and spray your plants until the fungus is gone.

Below you will find a list of fungal diseases and their symptoms:

Anthracnose

This fungal disease attacks vegetables such as beans, tomatoes, cucumbers, spinach, and watermelons. It is caused by a fungus and cool, wet weather. If your plants have anthracnose, their leaves will have black, tan, or red spots as well as lesions, and the leaves may become yellow and drop off. This is a fungal disease that tends to happen in late spring and early summer. Remove infected leaves and also collect and destroy any fallen leaves. Thin your plants so that air can circulate around them. You can spray the leaves with a copper or neem oil fungicide too.[30]

Black Spot

Black spot displays itself as black spots on leaves that go yellow and then die. If plants are in the shade and too close together, this can cause this fungal disease. To prevent black spot, ensure your plants have plenty of space so that air can circulate around them. Also, make sure you water your plants at the base, get rid of infected leaves, and spray them with a sulfur, copper, or neem oil fungicide if you notice this. Homemade baking soda fungicide works well against black spot too.[31]

---

[30] Image from https://www.gardentech.com/disease/anthracnose

[31] Image from https://www.gardentech.com/disease/black-spot

Blight

Blight refers to a specific symptom affecting plants in response to infection by a pathogenic organism. It is caused by fungi, which survive on infected plants or in plant debris. This can impact tomatoes, potatoes, and eggplants. There will be dark spots at the soil level of plants that will climb up toward the leaves of plants. If your plants have blight, act quickly to prevent it from spreading. Remove all affected leaves and burn them, or put them in a plastic bag and dispose of them in the trash. Blight is difficult to treat once it's established, but you can spray your plants with a copper fungicide in early stages of the disease.[32]

Clubroot

This is a soilborne fungal disease that can attack broccoli, cauliflower, cabbage, Brussels sprouts, radishes, and turnips. Plants don't grow well when they have it, and if you pull them up, they will have bulky roots. Leaves may go yellow and drop. Fungicides will not treat clubroot, and once it's in the soil, it can stay there for up to 20 years. It only attacks most brassicas, so you can rotate crops to get rid of it. Clubroot prefers acidic soil, so you can amend the pH level of your soil by adding hydrated lime, which will make the soil less acidic (increase its pH level). Determining the amounts of lime you need can be quite complicated, but your local garden center should be able to help you with that.[33]

Damping Off

This is a soilborne fungal disease that kills seedlings. Their stems and roots will rot if they have damping off, and healthy-looking seedlings can just keel over and die. It mostly happens when starting seeds indoors. There is no cure for plants that already have

---

[32] Image from https://www.planetnatural.com/pest-problem-solver/plant-disease/early-blight/

[33] Image from https://ucanr.edu/blogs/blogcore/postdetail.cfm?postnum=42974

damping off. However, you can reduce the chances of it happening it by starting seeds in fresh, soilless seed starting mix. Having proper ventilation also helps avoid damping off. A small fan or simply cracking the lid of your seed starting tray will suffice.

Downy Mildew

Downy mildew is an umbrella term for a large number of plant diseases. It is caused by a fungus-like organism called oomycetes or water molds. By the time plants show symptoms, it is already too late, so prevention is key.

This disease likes damp and cold conditions. It spreads through air and water splashing soil onto plants. Different plants can have different symptoms; however, one common symptom is yellow spots on the upper leaf surface between the leaf veins. These spots spread everywhere except the veins and eventually turn brown. Plants cannot photosynthesize on these yellow or brown spots, and when a leaf becomes totally brown, it drops. If a plant loses too many leaves, it will die.

Preventing downy mildew is much easier than controlling it. Water your plants at the base, and make sure they have good air circulation around them. Downy mildew spores overwinter in plant debris. After your crops are done, rake up all leaves and plant debris and dispose of them to help prevent the disease.

If your plants are seriously damaged, remove them and dispose of them in the trash. You can use copper or neem oil fungicides to control downy mildew in early stages. Homemade baking soda fungicide works well against downy mildew too.[34]

Gray Mold

This fungal disease is also known as botrytis blight. If your plants or their fruit appear to be misshapen and have gray fungal spores, this may be due to gray mold. Gray mold causes a dark brown to black blight of flowers, buds, leaves, and stems. Wounded and old

---

[34] Image from https://www.planetnatural.com/pest-problem-solver/plant-disease/downy-mildew/

plant tissue and flowers are easily infected by gray mold. Gray mold thrives in cool and wet conditions. However, many flowering plants can recover from gray mold when warm, dry conditions return.[35]

The best way to prevent gray mold is to space out plants so that they have good air circulation around them and can dry out after watering. You need to remove infected fruit, flowers, stems, or leaves from the plant and dispose of them, and if need be, thin out the plants so that plenty of air can circulate around them. You can use fungicides to control gray mold. Mycostop is an organic fungicide that works well against gray mold.

Powdery Mildew

Powdery mildew is a fungal disease that affects a wide variety of plants. There are many different species of powdery mildew, and each species attacks different plants. Plants that are commonly affected by powdery mildew include cucurbits (squash, pumpkins, cucumbers, melons), nightshades (tomatoes, eggplants, peppers), legumes (beans, peas), and roses.

Plants infected with powdery mildew look as if they have been dusted with flour. This disease usually starts off as circular, powdery white spots, which can appear on leaves, stems, and sometimes fruit. It usually covers the upper part of leaves.

To help prevent powdery mildew, water your plants from the base, and make sure they get enough sunlight and plenty of air can circulate around them. You can protect plants from powdery mildew by making a spray with 1 part milk and 2–3 parts water and spraying it on your plants every 10–14 days. This works especially well on cucumbers, zucchini, and melons.

If your plants have powdery mildew, you should remove all infected leaves, stems, and fruit and dispose of them. There are a few organic fungicides that work well against powdery mildew, including sulfur, lime-sulfur, neem oil, and potassium bicarbonate. Homemade baking soda fungicide works well too.

Rust

Rust is a common fungal disease spread by wind in wet conditions. Spores land on plants and breed. Plants that can be affected by rust include potatoes, sweet potatoes, carrots, onions, beans, peas, corn, eggplants, okra, artichokes, and asparagus. Plants affected

---

[35] Image from https://www.planetnatural.com/pest-problem-solver/plant-disease/gray-mold/

by rust will have rust-like spots on their leaves. This strips the nutrients out of plants and stunts their growth. It thrives in the summer when it's warm and humid. If your plants have rust, remove all infected parts and dispose of them. Also, clean away all debris in between plants to prevent rust from spreading. There are a lot of organic fungicides that can treat rust, so you can ask your local nursery what they have in stock. Neem oil fungicides work well against rust. Homemade baking soda fungicide works well too.[36]

Verticillium Wilt

Verticillium wilt is a soilborne fungal disease that enters plants through the roots. Plants' leaves will discolor and curl, then wilt, and plants may die when they have this. It can impact tomatoes, peppers, eggplants, cucumbers, pumpkins, and potatoes.

Verticillium wilt can be spread in contaminated soil, so if you suspect your plants might have it, be careful not to spread the soil from around the affected plants on tools or muddy boots. Weed control is important for prevention of this disease because some weeds are hosts, and in some cases, they will not show any visible signs of infection. There is no effective treatment for verticillium wilt. You will have to remove and dispose of infected plants. The best protection against verticillium wilt is growing plants with resistance or immunity to the disease.[37]

Bacterial Diseases

Plants are typically resistant to bacterial diseases. If your plants are healthy, they shouldn't get bacterial diseases. If pests have attacked plants' leaves or stems, then this could allow bacteria to enter and cause rot in the plants, and the plants may look slimy. There are no treatments for most bacterial diseases, so it is best to get rid of infected plants if this occurs and disinfect gardening tools to stop the bacteria from spreading.

Here is a list of bacterial diseases and their symptoms:

Bacterial Leaf Spot

Bacteria can get into the leaves of your plants and cause spots on the leaves, discoloration, and can cause

---

[36] Image from https://www.planetnatural.com/pest-problem-solver/plant-disease/common-rust/

[37] Image from https://content.ces.ncsu.edu/verticillium-wilt-of-tomato-and-eggplant

leaves to die. Bacterial leaf spot spreads in warm and wet conditions. Some of the plants commonly affected by this are lettuce, beets, eggplants, and peppers. You can pick off infected leaves, but if a plant has been systemically infected, you'll need to remove it and dispose of it in the trash. There are no treatments for bacterial leaf spot, but you can use copper fungicides to control the disease in early stages. Baking soda and neem oil fungicides will work too. Remove plant debris, and do not plant new crops where host plants were once growing.[38]

Bacterial Soft Rot

Bacterial soft rots are a group of diseases that cause more crop loss worldwide than any other bacterial disease. Bacterial soft rots affect a wide variety of plants, including lettuce, brassicas, cucurbits, tomatoes, peppers, potatoes, carrots, herbs, and more. Symptoms include wet, slimy, soft rot that affects all parts of vegetable crops, including heads, curds, edible roots, stems, and leaves. There is no treatment for bacterial soft rot. If your plants have this, immediately remove all infected plants or plant parts and dispose of them.[39]

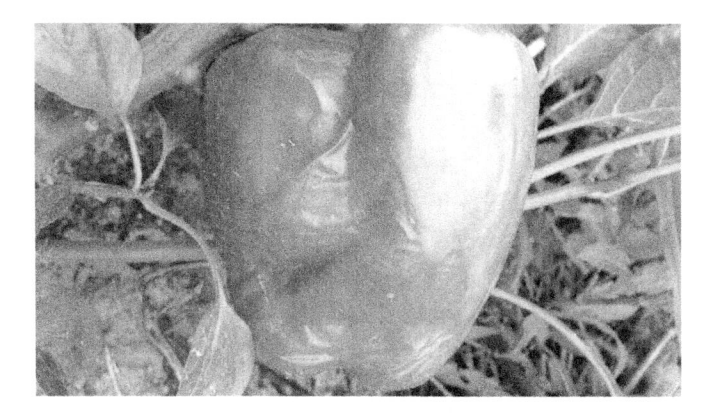

Black Rot

Black rot is a potentially lethal bacterial disease that affects most brassicas. Symptoms include light brown or yellow V-shaped lesions on leaves, and the leaves become brittle and dry with age. This disease thrives in warm and wet conditions. There are no treatments for black rot, but you can use copper fungicides to control the disease in early stages. You can remove infected leaves, but if a plant has been systemically infected, you'll need to remove the whole plant and dispose of it.[40]

---

[38] Image from https://www.gardening-knowhow.com/plant-problems/disease/bacterial-leaf-spot.htm

[39] Image from https://www.growingproduce.com/vegetables/more-vegetables/take-hard-line-bacterial-soft-rot-pepper/

[40] Image from https://ag.umass.edu/vegetable/fact-sheets/Brassicas-black-rot

Viral Diseases

Viral diseases are spread by insects, and you may notice yellow leaves that twist, crinkle, and then die. There is no treatment for viral diseases, so the best solution is to pull up infected plants, bag them up, and dispose of them in the trash. Viral diseases are spread by pests, so pest control is key to prevention. Make sure to weed your garden beds as well as the area around your greenhouse regularly because some weeds can be hosts for viral diseases.

Below is a list of viral diseases and their symptoms:

Mosaic Virus

Mosaic viruses are a group of viral diseases that are spread by aphids. There are a lot of different varieties of this virus that affect different plants, for example, cucumber mosaic virus, bean common mosaic virus, potato mosaic virus, and others. It can affect brassicas, cucurbits, beans, potatoes, tomatoes, peppers, celery, and other plants. If your plants have this, their leaves may curl, they won't grow well, and you won't get a bountiful harvest.

There is no treatment for mosaic virus, so you'll need to remove and dispose of any infected plants, including the roots, and also any plants near those affected. Since mosaic viruses are spread by aphids, pest control is key to prevention. Weeds can be hosts for mosaic viruses, so make sure to stay on top of weed control. You can also plant virus-resistant plant varieties in your garden.[41]

Tobacco Mosaic Virus

Tobacco mosaic virus is a tobamovirus. Other tobamoviruses include tomato mosaic virus and pepper mild mottle virus. Tobamoviruses are not transmitted by insects. They are highly infectious and very stable in the environment. They can survive on plants, root debris, seeds, tools, and contaminated clothing, which means they can be transmitted by a gardener who has touched an infected plant. It can affect eggplants, tomatoes, bok choy, bitter melon, long melon, Chinese mustard, snake beans, and Chinese cabbage. Symptoms include leaves having a mosaic pattern on them, mottling, leaf distortion, and sometimes leaves may die and fall off infected plants.

If your plants have this, remove and dispose of them. Burn them if you can, or double bag them and dispose of them in the trash. To help prevent this virus, do not smoke and handle plants or allow tobacco products near the garden. If you notice your plants have this, avoid handling other plants, remove and dispose of infected plants as soon as possible, wash your hands, sanitize your tools, wash your clothes, take a shower, and change your clothes before handling other plants.

---

[41] Image from https://www.planetnatural.com/pest-problem-solver/plant-disease/mosaic-virus/

Tomato Spotted Wilt Virus

This virus is spread by thrips. It can affect peppers, tomatoes, eggplants, lettuce, celery, peas, potatoes, and sweet basil. Plants infected with this will have bronzing of the upper sides of young leaves, which later develop distinct necrotic spots. Other symptoms include ring spots, line patterns, mottling, and chlorotic blotches on leaves. If your plants have this, remove and dispose of them. Make sure to control thrips and weeds to help prevent it from happening in the future.

Other Diseases

Some diseases can be caused by environmental factors, such as drought, freezing, and other stressors. One of the most common diseases of this type is blossom-end rot.

Blossom-End Rot

Blossom-end rot is an environmental problem, which is typically caused by uneven watering or calcium deficiency. This can mean your tomatoes, peppers, eggplants, or cucumbers have rotten bottoms. Blossom end rot will not spread from plant to plant. To prevent blossom end rot, try to keep your soil evenly moist, and add bone meal or oyster shells to your soil to enrich it with calcium.[42]

Disease Prevention

Prevention is better than cure, and that's true with plant health as well. Below are some things you can do to help prevent diseases in your garden:

1. Water plants at the base, and avoid splashing water on leaves or splashing soil on plants. Water plants in the morning to allow any water splashes to dry. This will help prevent fungal diseases.
2. Ensure your plants have sufficient airflow around them and get a good amount of sunlight. If the environment around plants is dark and moist, this is an ideal breeding ground for diseases.
3. Clear any weeds or dead plants because they can house pests and diseases. If you notice any leaves are diseased, remove them and dispose of them in the trash. Do not put them in compost.
4. Wash your hands and tools in between tending to different crops so that you don't spread diseases like the mosaic virus unknowingly.
5. If you think you have experienced damping off with seedlings, then get rid of the soil they were grown in and start again with fresh, soilless seed starting mix.
6. Check any plants you purchase for signs of diseases before you plant them in your garden.
7. Purchase good quality plants and seeds from reputable suppliers that look healthy (and not spindly).

---

[42] Image from https://morningchores.com/blossom-end-rot/

8. You can also purchase disease-resistant varieties of plants. The seed catalog will generally let you know which varieties are disease resistant. Sometimes when you buy disease-resistant plants, they will have abbreviations such as F2 or F3, which means Fusarium resistance. N stands for nematode resistance. AB means resistant to early blight, and LB means resistant to late blight. PB is resistant to powdery mildew, and DM resistant to downy mildew. A means anthracnose resistant. S means scab resistant. BMV is bean mosaic virus resistant.

9. Rotate crops (put your crops in different parts of the garden each year), and avoid rotating plants from the same family, for example, tomatoes, eggplants, and peppers or cabbage, broccoli, and cauliflower. This will be covered in more detail in the next section.

10. Don't transplant your plants into garden beds too early if it's still cold. They won't grow as well and may be more prone to pests and diseases.

11. Mulch your garden beds and raised beds because this will prevent soil from splashing onto the plants. It will also help retain moisture and reduce weeds.

12. Try to prevent pests from damaging your plants because disease-causing organisms can get inside plants through holes and cuts and infect them.

Crop Rotation

Crop rotation means planting different crops sequentially on the same plot of land, and it helps improve soil health and fertility, optimize nutrients in the soil as well as combat pests and weeds. By rotating crops, you can also prevent the buildup of large populations of soilborne pathogens. If you kept the same crop in the soil year after year (a monoculture), the pathogens would build up, and you would have a lot of losses to your crop. Growing the same crop year after year in the same soil allows pests and diseases to get really well established there. It would also deplete the soil of the nutrients that type of crop needs. Planting crops year after year would mean that they would grow slowly and be not as healthy, and you'd get less yield from them.

But if you change your crops to something that isn't a host for that soilborne pathogen, the pathogen will die out, and you'll get a better yield come harvest time. Many soil pathogens die out after a few years if there are no suitable hosts, so rotating crops can help eliminate pathogens in the soil.

It's not a good idea to rotate crops that belong to the same family, as they are often affected by the same pathogens. The term "plant family" is used to describe fairly wide groups of plants with similar characteristics. The most commonly grown vegetables belong to the following families:

- Amaryllodaceae (lily or onion family, also called alliums)
- Apiaceae or Umbelliferae (carrot family, also called umbellifers)
- Brassicaceae (brassica or cabbage family, also called brassicas)
- Cucurbitaceae (gourd or squash family, also called cucurbits)
- Fabaceae (legume or pea family, also called legumes)

- Solanaceae (nightshade family or simply nightshades)

Plants in the onion family (alliums) include onions, garlic, leeks, chives, shallots, and other species within the Allium genus. The carrot family includes carrots, celery, chervil, cilantro (coriander), cumin, dill, fennel, lovage, cow parsley, parsley, parsnips, and more. Brassicas include broccoli, Brussels sprouts, cabbage, cauliflower, collards, kale, mustard, radishes, and more. The gourd family includes zucchini, pumpkins as well as summer and winter squash, which most people would class as vegetables. But the family also includes melons, more commonly considered a fruit, as well as cucumbers, which lie somewhere in between. The legume family includes peas and beans, although lentils are also classed within the same group. And finally, the nightshade family includes tomatoes, peppers, eggplants, and potatoes.

For example, broccoli, cabbage, turnips, and mustard are all part of the brassica family, so do not rotate these because it won't help reduce pathogens in the soil. Your vegetables would be more prone to black rot, fusarium wilt, and clubroot.

Some pathogens, such as *Rhizoctoinia solani*, *Sclerotium rolfsii*, and *Pythium* species, attack a lot of different vegetables, so if you suspect you have these pathogens in your soil, it would be best to include small grains in your crop rotation.

If you're growing potatoes and they got potato rot, this will also affect other plants in the nightshade family, such as eggplants, tomatoes, and peppers. If your potatoes were impacted by Colorado potato beetles and you planted potatoes there for another year, the beetles would multiply and lay even more eggs. Whereas if you planted a completely different plant from a different family in there, potato beetles would die off and you'd stop that cycle.

Some pests will stay in the soil for 5 years or more, so rotating crops isn't going to get rid of them. Clubroot spores can stay in the soil for up to 20 years, and white rot (which affects alliums) can survive for up to 40 years.

It's good practice to rotate crops, and even though crop rotation won't eliminate all pathogens and prevent all diseases, it's still a good method of disease prevention and managing soil fertility. It does take a bit of planning and organizing, but it is well worth it. When you rotate crops, different crops improve the soil and give it nutrients that other plants can use, such as legumes fixing nitrogen in the soil.

A full crop rotation cycle lasts 3 to 4 years; however, this is not really practical for greenhouses, especially small ones. The good news is that even a single year's rotation can help eliminate pests and diseases and helps spread out the demand on specific soil nutrients that different crops need. Even if you have a small greenhouse with just a couple of garden beds, you could swap plants growing in them, and it would still be better than growing the same plants year after year. You can plan out your crop rotation cycle and keep track of this in a garden journal with a sketch as to your current year and next year's planting. I have created a garden journal that will help you keep all the important information about your garden and plants in one convenient place. If you'd like to find out more about it, please check page 5 of this book.

Companion Planting for Disease Management

As we now know, companion planting is about growing certain plants near each other so that plants are healthier and can produce a better yield. They can support each other physically with shade or actual support to grow up like a trellis, and they can enrich the soil with nutrients. They can help one another in many ways, and one of them is controlling pests and diseases.

Herbs are excellent companion plants because they help repel pests, which can spread diseases and also damage your plants and make them more vulnerable to diseases.

Asparagus and tomatoes make good companions because tomatoes produce solanine, which is toxic to asparagus beetles, and asparagus produces a substance that deters nematodes, which can damage tomato roots.

Planting garlic, onions, borage, and horseradish among your vegetables can help make them more disease resistant. Garlic contains sulfur, which is a naturally occurring fungicide. If you plant chives near apple trees, they will prevent scab, and if you plant them near rose bushes, they will help prevent black spot. If you put onions with strawberries, it will make strawberries more disease resistant. Borage is good for preventing diseases with strawberries and tomatoes. Horseradish makes potatoes more disease resistant and also repels Colorado potato beetles. Putting chamomile next to any plants or shrubs that are ailing may help heal them, as they are naturally anti-fungal.

I remember I used to get quite a lot of ants in my first greenhouse, and then aphids came to join the party. They often go hand in hand because ants like honeydew that is left from aphids sucking the sap out of leaves and stems. Ants can damage things like corn, cucumbers, watermelons, potatoes, and okra. First, we sprayed plants that had aphids on them with a hose to remove them. Then we made a neem oil spray to spray on plants infested by aphids. We knew that once the aphids are gone, the ants would go too. We sprayed the infested plants every 3–4 days for a few weeks, just to be sure we dealt with the infestation, and aphids indeed disappeared. Shortly after, ants were gone too.

Key takeaways from this chapter:

1. Common pests include aphids, caterpillars, carrot rust flies, codling moths, Colorado potato beetles, Mexican bean beetles, slugs, snails, tomato or tobacco hornworms, and whiteflies.
2. You can make organic sprays to repel pests with chili peppers, garlic, neem oil, vegetable oil, and soap.
3. You can nip off leaves and buds that show evidence of pests and/or diseases and dispose of them in the trash. You can also pick off pests by hand.
4. Some insects, such as ladybugs and lacewings, are natural predators to pests and will eat them. You can attract predatory insects by planting flowers and flowering herbs.
5. Plant diseases can be caused by fungi, bacteria, or viruses.
6. To prevent diseases, water your plants at the base, and avoid getting water on the leaves or splashing them with soil. You can thin your crops out to

improve air circulation. If your plants have signs of diseases, you may need to remove and dispose of diseased parts, like leaves, or sometimes whole plants. Check plants from nurseries before buying them. Buy disease-resistant plant seeds. You will find code letters on them that indicate which diseases they are resistant to.

7. Crop rotation helps reduce pests and pathogens in the soil. Rotate crops (put your crops in different parts of the garden each year) and avoid rotating plants from the same family, for example, tomatoes, eggplants, and peppers or cabbage, broccoli, and cauliflower. If you plant crops from different families every year, pathogens in the soil will die off because they won't have any suitable hosts.

8. You can use companion planting to help repel pests and improve the disease resistance of your plants.

The next chapter will give you information on how you can tell if it's the right time to harvest your vegetables, fruits, and herbs, the signs to look out for, and how to harvest them. It will also cover how you can store your harvest to get the most out of it.

Chapter 8: Time to Harvest the Bounty

So, you've started your garden and took good care of your plants during the growing season. You've ensured that your soil is as healthy as possible, and you've been watering and weeding your garden dutifully. You've done your best to control pests and attract beneficial insects and pollinators to your garden. All of these things should have given your vegetables, fruits, and herbs the optimum conditions to thrive. It's now time for the exciting part of harvesting your bounty!

So, this chapter will cover when you should harvest your crops and how you can tell they're ready to harvest. It will also cover how you should store your harvest to keep it fresh and preserved.

When and How to Harvest Your Vegetables

While seed packets provide information on how long it takes for plants to reach maturity—and this is a helpful guide—there are numerous factors that can change this, including the weather, the quality of your soil, whether your plants got enough water, and so on. But vegetables themselves give some clues as to whether they are mature, and this chapter will help you learn about these.

Some vegetables taste best when they are tender and immature. Things like peas, salad greens, zucchini, cucumbers, beans, potatoes, radishes, cabbage, broccoli, cauliflower, summer squash, and turnips fall into this category. Other plants need to ripen on the vine, such as tomatoes, melons, and winter squash. Most herbs should be harvested before they flower because when they do, they lose their flavor.

It is important to regularly check whether your vegetables are ready to be harvested because if you leave some vegetables for too long, they can become tough or overripe. For example, beans can become tough if left for too long, and zucchini can become overripe.

Before you start harvesting, there are certain tools that will come in handy. These include a clean, food-safe container that you can put your harvest in—this could be a stainless steel bowl, a plastic bowl, or a basket. You will need scissors or pruners and food-safe wipes or soap to be able to clean your tools. Ensure that you have washed your hands and tools before harvesting to avoid spreading any diseases.

For lettuce, kale, and peas, you can pinch off leaves and peas by hand. With lettuce and other leafy vegetables that sprout from the center of the plant, if you're just taking a few leaves and not harvesting the entire thing, then take the outer leaves first so that the plant can continue to grow. If something doesn't come off easily, you can use scissors or a knife. If you have root crops, like potatoes or beets, then you may need to use a fork to harvest them. With herbs and salad leaves, you can use scissors to snip off the leaves, and it's best to take the leaves from around the base of the plant first so that the plant can continue to grow.

Typically, it's best to harvest plants when the temperature is lower—in the morning or later in the evening—because plants will be less stressed. After the morning dew has dried is a good time to harvest. If you were to pick vegetables in midday heat, it can cause leafy vegetables to wilt. Don't harvest vegetables if it's wet because you could easily spread fungal diseases in wet conditions.

You can harvest daily. If you have too much produce, you can store it (this will be covered later in this chapter) or share it with friends, family, and neighbors. Storing your harvest is not the only way to preserve it, of course. You can preserve your harvest with pickling, canning, making jams, freezing, and drying, and I could write a book about it. In fact, I did, and I'd like you to have it for free as a way of saying thanks for purchasing this book. To get your free eBook about 5 easy ways to preserve your harvest, please scan the QR code on page 4 with your phone camera or send me an email to maxbarnesbooks@gmail.com and I will send you the free eBook.

Below you will find information on how to harvest different vegetables:

Arugula: Cut off leaves when they have reached 2–3 inches (5–7.5 cm). Younger leaves taste best. Older leaves can be bitter.

Asparagus: It's ready to harvest when the spears are 6–8 inches (15–20 cm) long and as thick as your pinky finger. Cut the spears with a knife at soil level. Usually, you can harvest asparagus for 4–8 weeks. If you grow asparagus from seed, it can take 3 years before the plant is productive.

Beans: They're ready to harvest when they're as thick as a pencil and you can easily snap a pod in two. You should aim to harvest every day or two.

Beets: They should be dug up when their roots are 1.5–2.5 inches (4–6.5 cm) in diameter. You can also harvest and eat the green tops and have them in salads, steamed, or stir-fried.

Bok choy: When it's 12 inches (30 cm), you can either take the whole plant and cut it with a knife at the roots, or take outer leaves with a knife, or cut all the stems to about an inch (2.5 cm) in height, and new leaves will then start to appear.

Broccoli: When it's 3–6 inches (7.5–15 cm) in diameter, cut the stalk 6 inches (15 cm) below the head. Broccoli grown at home won't get to the sizes that you find in a supermarket.

Brussels sprouts: When the sprouts are 1–1.5 inches (2.5–4 cm) in diameter, start harvesting at the bottom of the stalk where the sprouts are more mature, then move up. You can twist them off or cut them off with a knife.

Cabbage: When the head is a bit bigger than a softball, harvest the cabbage. If you leave it too long, it may split open.

Carrots: Harvest when they're 1 inch (2.5 cm) in diameter.

Cauliflower: It needs to be watched carefully, and you should harvest it before the head separates, or turns yellow, or gets brown spots. Cut with a knife below the head, ensuring you have some leaves attached to stop it from drying out.

Chard: When the leaves are 6 inches (15 cm) long, you can snip them off from the outside of the plant.

Corn: When silks go dry and brown (about 3 weeks after forming) and if the ear (the spiked part of the corn plant that contains kernels) feels rounded, it can be harvested. If it tapers and feels thin at the tip, it's not ready. If you nick a kernel with your finger, it should be succulent and have a milky substance come out. Pick corn in the morning, and place it in the fridge until cooking.

Cucumbers: Harvest them when they're 2–6 inches (5–15 cm) long. The skin should be dark, green, and glossy. If it's dull or yellow, the cucumber is past its best.

Eggplants: Harvest them when their skin is even colored and glossy. If it's dull and the eggplant is soft, it's overripe. Cut eggplants off a plant using a pruner or knife.

Garlic: If you have planted garlic in the spring, it will be ready mid-summer to early fall. If you've planted it in the fall, it will be ready in early summer. You can tell if it's the right time to harvest garlic when the leaves have turned yellow. You should carefully dig up garlic using a fork, being careful not to bruise or damage it. Then garlic needs to be dried in a single layer in the sun, ideally under a cloche, or in a greenhouse or a shed for 2–4 weeks. When the leaves are dry, you can cut off the stalks.

Kale: When the leaves are 6–8 inches (15–20 cm), they're ready to harvest. You can snap them off or use a knife. Harvest the outer leaves at the base of the plant first.

Kohlrabi: When the globes are 2 inches (5 cm) in diameter, they're ready to be harvested. Cut the globe at the root with a knife.

Leeks: Harvest when they're 1 inch (2.5 cm) in diameter. Use a garden fork to loosen the soil, then pull them up from the ground. You can leave leeks in the ground over winter and harvest when needed.

Lettuce: Harvest when it's about 6 inches (15 cm) in diameter. Use a knife to sever the head from the roots. With lettuce leaves, you can harvest them when they are 3–4 inches (7.5–10 cm) long by cutting them off with scissors from the outside. Lettuce tastes best early in the day. If you do pick it later in the day, refresh the leaves in cold water for 30 minutes, dry them with paper towels, then place in a plastic bag in the fridge.

Melons: With cantaloupes, they're ready to harvest when the stem pulls easily from the melon and they smell sweet when sniffed. With honeydews, they're ready to harvest when the flower end is softer and the rind is white or yellow. Cut melons from the vine with a knife.

Mustard greens: Use scissors or a knife to harvest the leaves when they are young, tender, and mild. Harvest leaves from the outside of the plant.

Onions: When they're about 1–2 inches (2.5–5 cm) in diameter and when more than $\frac{2}{3}$ of the tops have dried and fallen over, they're ready to be harvested. You should be able to pull them from the ground with your hands in most cases. You can use a fork to help if they're not coming out easily. Hang them up in the sun or somewhere dry for 1–2 weeks. When the necks are dry, trim the roots and store in a cool, dry space.

Parsnips: Harvest after a few frosts for sweeter tasting parsnips. You can also leave them in the ground over winter and harvest them in the spring. Cover them with a thick layer of straw or organic mulch if you leave them over winter. To harvest, use a garden fork to loosen soil, then pull them out. Cut the foliage to ¼ of an inch (6 mm). Store in the fridge or a root cellar.

Peas: You can pull a pod from the vine and do a taste test to see if they're ready. Snip the pods off the vine with scissors or fingers. Harvest daily or every other day. If overripe peas are left on the vine, the vine will not produce anymore.

Peppers: You can harvest them ripe or unripe. Use scissors to cut them off because if you try to twist them off, you will damage the plant. You can pick green peppers, and the plant will continue to produce them. If you let peppers ripen on the vine, the peppers will be sweeter, but you won't get as many. With hot peppers, they're hotter when they're green rather than red. It can be worth wearing gloves when handling them because they can burn your hands. Also, don't rub your eyes when harvesting peppers—wash your hands first.

Potatoes: With new potatoes, they're ready to harvest once they've flowered (usually 6–8 weeks after planting). With other potatoes, leave them in the ground for 2 weeks after the plants have died back. Carefully dig them up so that you don't damage them. They can be stored in a dark and dry place for 2 weeks.

Pumpkins: When a pumpkin has a deep color, the stem has started to dry, and the rind cannot be dented when pressed with a thumbnail, it's ready to be harvested. Use a knife to sever it from the vine. Leave 3 inches (7.5 cm) of the stem attached, and don't carry pumpkins by the stem because you don't want to break it. Let them cure in a well-ventilated place for 10 days.

Radishes: Harvest radishes when they're about 1 inch (2.5 cm) in diameter. If you leave them for too long, they'll be hot, sharp, and pithy. Use a garden fork to loosen soil and pull them up.

Rutabagas: These are ready to harvest when their roots are 4–5 inches (10–12.5 cm) in diameter. Cool weather makes them taste better, so allow them a few frosts. Dig up the roots with a garden fork. Wash off the soil, dry the roots quickly, and store in a root cellar or a fridge.

Shallots: They are ready to harvest when they're 1–1.5 inches (2.5–4 cm) in diameter and the tops have turned brown and flopped over. Store them in a dry place for a week.

Spinach: When the leaves are 3 inches (7.5 cm) long, you can harvest them from the outside of the plant. Tender leaves are more flavorsome and easier to pinch off with fingers. When spinach flowers, stop harvesting it.

Squash: Harvest when small and tender. If the skin toughens, it will be very seedy. Cut squash from the vine with a knife. For winter squash, when the vine shrivels and dries and the rind is hard, it's ready to harvest. Let the squash cure in the sun for 10 days, don't get it wet, and bring it indoors if it looks like it's going to rain.

Sweet potatoes: When the foliage turns yellow, your sweet potatoes are ready to harvest. Lift them from the ground carefully with a garden fork. Cure them in the sun for a day, then place in the shade for 7–10 days.

Tomatoes: They are ready to harvest when fully vine ripened but still firm. You can use scissors to snip them off the plant. If you have unripe tomatoes but you're expecting a frost, then bring them indoors, and wrap the tomatoes in newspaper with space between them for air to circulate.

Turnips: Harvest when the roots are 2–3 inches (5–7.5 cm) in diameter. Turnips have edible foliage too.

Watermelons: Watermelons are ready to harvest when the rind underneath goes from greenish white to a cream or yellow color. Cut watermelons from the vine with a knife, leaving 2 inches (5 cm) of stem attached.

Storing Your Harvest

If you're planning on storing your harvested produce away for later use, you can lightly rinse greens and wrap them in a paper towel to store in the fridge. With other vegetables that you harvest, such as tomatoes, peppers, or onions, don't wash these until you need to use them. This will help prevent them from spoiling.

If you want to store vegetables and fruits to eat later, you can store some for months under the right conditions. You need to select vegetables and fruits that are unblemished and check them regularly to make sure any damaged or diseased vegetables or fruits are removed so that they won't spoil the remainder. If you have one rotten piece of fruit or a rotten vegetable, it can ruin all the rest. You can buy wooden crate storage boxes or use shallow cardboard boxes. If you stack these, ensure that there is space between them for air to circulate.

Different vegetables and fruits need different storage conditions. Temperature and humidity are the most important factors to consider. You've probably seen recommendations like "store in a cool, dry place". But exactly does "cool, dry place" mean? There are three combinations for long-term storage:

- Cool and dry (50–60°F (10–15°C) and 60% relative humidity)
- Cold and dry (32–40°F (0–4°C) and 65% relative humidity)
- Cold and moist (32-40°F (0–4°C) and 95% relative humidity)

The ideal temperature for cold conditions is 32°F (0°C). This temperature is not easy to attain in most homes, however. You can expect shortened shelf life for your vegetables the more storage conditions deviate from the ideal temperature. Shelf life shortens approximately 25% for every 10°F (5.5°C) increase in temperature.

Basements are generally cool and dry. If you decide to store vegetables in your basement, they will need some ventilation. Harvested vegetables still "breathe" and need oxygen to maintain their freshness. Also, make sure to protect your stored produce from rodents.

Refrigerators are generally cold and dry. This works well for long-term storage of garlic and onions, but not much else. If you put vegetables in plastic bags in the fridge, this will create too much humidity, which can lead to the growth of mold and bacteria. You can put vegetables in perforated plastic bags, and this will create cold and moist conditions, but only for a moderate amount of time.

Root cellars are generally cold and moist. If you store vegetables in a cellar, they'll need some ventilation and protection from rodents. You can use materials such as straw, hay, or wood shavings for insulation. If you decide to use insulation, make sure that it's clean.

You can store carrots, potatoes, and beets. To do so, ensure that you have removed the leafy tops off carrots and beets. Don't wrap them, and place them in a single layer. You can cover them with a layer of sand to stop them from going rubbery. You can store potatoes in hessian or paper sacks. It's good to harvest potatoes when the weather is dry and then leave them in the sun to dry. Ensure that mud is removed from potatoes to prevent mold. Make sure to store potatoes somewhere dark to stop them from going green.

Most vegetables prefer cold and moist conditions, so a root cellar is the perfect place for long-term storage of most vegetables. Storage conditions for different vegetables and fruits will be covered below.

Cool and dry conditions are suitable for some pumpkins, zucchini, winter squash, and onions.

Cold and moist conditions are suitable for root crops, such as potatoes, carrots, beets, radishes, turnips, and parsnips, as well as asparagus, beans, broccoli, cabbage, cauliflower, corn, spinach, and peas. Produce that needs cold and moist conditions can be stored in the fridge, but it will last less because refrigerators tend to dry things out.

Some vegetables, such as cucumbers, peppers, tomatoes, and eggplants, require cool and moist storage conditions (55°F or 13°C and 90–95% relative humidity). It's difficult to maintain these conditions in a typical home, so you can expect to keep vegetables that require such storage conditions for only a short period of time.

Berries can't be stored for long. Never rinse berries before storage because it will wash off the thin protective epidermal layer. Place them on a paper towel in a tightly covered container, and store them in the fridge for 2–3 days.

If you want to store onions or shallots, these need to be dried, plaited, and stored in a dry place. You can cut the tops off and hang them in tights or netting.

Any leafy vegetables don't store well, and you should ideally eat these within a few days of harvesting them.

Below you will find a table with storage conditions for a variety of different vegetables and fruits as well as their approximate storage life:

Produce	Temperature	Relative humidity (percent)	Approximate storage life
Berries			
— Strawberries	32°F (0°C)	90–95	3–7 days
Vegetables			
Asparagus	32–35°F (0–1.5°C)	95–100	2–3 weeks
Beans, green or snap	40–45°F (4–7°C)	95	7–10 days
Beets, topped	32°F (0°C)	98–100	4–6 months
Broccoli	32°F (0°C)	95–100	10–14 days
Brussels sprouts	32°F (0°C)	95–100	3–5 weeks
Cabbage, early	32°F (0°C)	98–100	3–6 weeks
Cabbage, late	32°F (0°C)	98–100	5–6 months

Produce	Temperature	Relative humidity (percent)	Approximate storage life
Carrots	32°F (0°C)	98–100	7–9 months
Cauliflower	32°F (0°C)	95–98	3–4 weeks
Celeriac	32°F (0°C)	97–99	6–8 months
Celery	32°F (0°C)	98–100	2–3 months
Chard	32°F (0°C)	95–100	10–14 days
Corn, sweet	32°F (0°C)	95–98	5–8 days
Cucumbers	50–55°F (10–13°C)	95	10–14 days
Eggplant	46–54°F (8–12°C)	90–95	1 week
Garlic	32°F (0°C)	65–70	6–7 months
Horseradish	30–32°F (–1 to 0°C)	98–100	10–12 months
Kale	32°F (0°C)	95–100	2–3 weeks
Leeks	32°F (0°C)	95–100	2–3 months
Lettuce	32°F (0°C)	98–100	2–3 weeks
Onions, green	32°F (0°C)	95–100	3–4 weeks
Onions, dry	32°F (0°C)	65–70	1–8 months
Onion sets	32°F (0°C)	65–70	6–8 months
Parsley	32°F (0°C)	95–100	2–2.5 months
Parsnips	32°F (0°C)	98–100	4–6 months
Peas, green	32°F (0°C)	95–98	1–2 weeks
Peppers, chili (dry)	32–50°F (0–10°C)	60–70	6 months
Peppers, sweet	45–55°F (7–13°C)	90–95	2–3 weeks
Potatoes, early crop	40°F (4°C)	90–95	4–5 months
Potatoes, late crop	38–40°F (3–4°C)	90–95	5–10 months
Pumpkins	50–55°F (10–13°C)	50–70	2–3 months
Radishes, spring	32°F (0°C)	95–100	3–4 weeks
Radishes, winter	32°F (0°C)	95–100	2–4 months
Rhubarb	32°F (0°C)	95–100	2–4 weeks
Rutabagas	32°F (0°C)	98–100	4–6 months
Spinach	32°F (0°C)	95–100	10–14 days
Squashes, summer	41–50°F (5–10°C)	95	1–2 weeks
Squashes, winter	50°F (10°C)	50–70	1–6 months

Produce	Temperature	Relative humidity (percent)	Approximate storage life
Sweet potatoes	55–60°F (13–16°C)	85–90	4–7 months
Tomatoes mature, green	55–70°F (13–21°C)	90–95	1–3 weeks
Tomatoes firm, ripe	55–70°F (13–21°C)	90–95	4–7 days
Turnips	32°F (0°C)	95	4–5 months

I think there is no better thing than eating vegetables and fruits you have grown yourself in the garden. It is wonderful going out into the garden with a basket and picking fresh, organic vegetables that you've grown yourself, gently rinsing them, and then cooking them for an evening meal. I still remember when we harvested produce from our garden for the first time and I roasted the vegetables and made a vegetable lasagna with rich, tangy tomato sauce between the layers and had it with a side salad. To this day, it may be one of the best meals I've ever had. The taste was phenomenal, and I felt so much pride in knowing that I've grown these tasty vegetables from seed and have nurtured them into something that fed me and my family very well. We had so much lovely produce! We shared it with family and friends and made things like pickles and chutneys. I adore gardening and getting all the lovely rewards from it, and greenhouse gardening allows us to grow a variety of delicious vegetables, fruits, and herbs year-round.

Key takeaways from this chapter:

1. Some vegetables taste best when they are tender and immature, such as salad greens, zucchini, cucumbers, potatoes, radishes, cabbage, broccoli, cauliflower, spinach, turnips, oregano, and basil.
2. With salad or leafy greens, take leaves from the outer side of the plant so that the plant can continue to grow.
3. Harvest vegetables in the morning, ideally after the morning dew has dried.
4. Never harvest when it's wet because you could spread fungal diseases.
5. You can harvest daily.
6. Things like broccoli and cauliflower that you grow in your garden won't be as large as the ones you might find in a supermarket, but they'll be tastier.
7. When harvesting sprouts, start at the bottom of the stalk.
8. Garlic and onions need to be cured in the sun for 2 weeks.
9. You can leave parsnips and some other root vegetables in the ground over winter and dig them up when required.
10. With herbs, wrap them in a paper towel and place in a plastic bag in the fridge to reduce wilting.
11. Don't refrigerate tomatoes.

The next chapter will look at plant profiles of different vegetables and fruits. This will help you when selecting the best type of plants to grow in your garden. This chapter will give you information on how to start different plants, how much light they require, what conditions they prefer, how much water and fertilization they need, and when they should be harvested. This will help you make better choices before selecting plants to grow. It will cover a variety of vegetables, fruits, herbs, and flowers.

Chapter 9: Plant Profiles

This chapter is here to help you make informed decisions about what plants you could grow in your garden. You will know what type of soil and what growing conditions different plants prefer, how to start them, their sun requirements, how much water they need, how often they need to be fertilized, whether they need any special care, like support or pruning, and other important information regarding growing different types of plants.

All plants can be classified as annuals, biennials, or perennials—these terms are related to the life cycle of plants. Annuals complete their entire life cycle in just one year. They go from seed to plant to flower and to seed again during that one year. Only the seed survives to start the next generation, and the rest of the plant dies. Biennials take up to two years to complete their life cycle. They produce vegetation in the first year, and in the second year, they produce flowers and seeds that go on to produce the next generation. Many vegetables are biennials but are often grown as annuals. Perennials live more than two years—from three years to hundreds of years. The above-ground portion of perennial plants may die in the winter and come back from the roots the following year. Some plants may retain foliage throughout the winter. Trees and shrubs are perennials.

This chapter covers 20 vegetables, 3 fruits, 6 herbs, and 3 flowers. Clearly, this chapter won't cover every type of plant you may wish to grow in your garden, but for a beginner just starting out, it will give you some good pointers as to some of the more common plants you can grow in your garden and what to expect from them.

Vegetables

Beets (Beetroot)

Beets prefer well-drained soils with pH levels between 6.0 and 7.0.

Beets are biennial plants grown as annuals. They don't like to be transplanted, so you'll need to direct sow them. Plant the seeds ½ inch (1.2 cm) deep. Beets need 3–4 inches (7.5–10 cm) of space between plants for smaller varieties and 6 inches (15 cm) for larger ones. Rows should be spaced 12–18 inches (30–45 cm) apart.

Beets can be grown in full or partial sun, and they will need at least 6 hours of sunlight per day. They are a cool-season crop, and they prefer temperatures around 50–85°F (10–30°C). Beets need 1 inch (2.5 cm) of water per week. It's a good idea to use either time-based (slow-release) fertilizer or compost to enrich the soil when they sprout and then fertilize them again with a liquid fertilizer about 5 weeks after that when they break the soil surface. Beets are a root vegetable, so they need a fertilizer that is low in nitrogen but high in phosphorus and potassium.

Beets typically take 6–9 weeks to get ready for harvest after germination. You can also harvest beet greens to use in salads—their tender leaves taste delicious. You can start harvesting greens when leaves are a few inches long by cutting the outer leaves only and leaving the small inner foliage to grow, which you can harvest later.

Broccoli

Broccoli grows best in well-drained soils with a pH level between 6.0 and 6.8.

Broccoli is a biennial plant grown as an annual. You can start broccoli in containers or direct sow it—sow the seeds ½ inch (0.6 cm) deep. Give them plenty of light, and water them regularly. They will germinate in 1–2 weeks. You can transplant them to your garden beds once they are 3–7 inches (7.5–18 cm) tall and have 2–4 true leaves. Broccoli needs 18 inches (45 cm) of space between plants and 18–24 inches (45–60 cm) of space between rows.

Broccoli needs full sun and at least 6 hours of sunlight per day. It's a cool-season crop, and it grows best in temperatures between 65 and 75°F (18–24°C). It needs 1–2 inches (2.5–5 cm) of water per week. Fertilize broccoli 3 weeks after transplanting seedlings into garden beds and then every 2–3 weeks after that. You can use a low-nitrogen fertilizer, but balanced fertilizers work well too. You may need to prune them if you notice vigorous growth. You'll need to pinch out newly developing side shoots, and you can also cut away wilting leaves from sides. But don't go too hard on it—avoid excessive pruning.

Broccoli will be ready to harvest in 60–90 days after seeding. Look out for light green buds, and cut them with 4–5 inches (10–12.5 cm) of stem, but leave the outer leaves intact because they are going to encourage new growth.

Cabbage

Cabbage prefers well-drained soil with a pH level between 6 and 7.

Cabbage is a biennial plant grown as an annual. Cabbage can be direct sown or started in containers. Plant the seeds ¼ to ½ inch (0.6–1.2 cm) deep. Some cabbage varieties can require up to 24 inches (60 cm) of spacing between plants; however, most compact varieties need 1 foot (30 cm) of space, and most larger varieties need 18 inches (45 cm) of space between plants and 12–24 inches (30–60 cm) of space between rows. You can check the seed packet for spacing requirements for the specific variety you're growing.

Cabbage needs full sun with 6–8 hours of sunlight per day. Cabbage is a cool-season crop, and it grows best in temperatures between 60 and 65°F (15–18°C) and no higher than 75°F (24°C). Cabbage needs 1–2 inches (2.5–5 cm) of water per week. You can fertilize cabbage with a balanced liquid fertilizer every 2–3 weeks. Compost tea works great for cabbage.

Cabbage generally takes around 70–80 days to reach maturity; however, some varieties can take up to 4–6 months to grow, depending on the type. Harvest them once they have reached the size you want and formed a firm head. To harvest, cut each cabbage head at the base with a sharp knife, remove any yellow leaves, but keep loose green leaves because they provide protection in storage, and immediately bring the head indoors, or place it in shade.

Carrots

Carrots prefer well-drained soil with pH levels between 6.0 and 7.0.

Carrots are biennial plants grown as annuals. They don't like to be transplanted, so it's best to direct sow them. Carrot seeds should be placed ¼ to ½ inch (0.6–1.2 cm) below the surface of the soil. Carrots need 2–3 inches (5–7.5 cm) of space between them and 1 foot (30 cm) of space between rows.

Carrots like full sun. They need at least 6 hours of sunlight per day. Carrots are a cool-season crop, and the ideal temperature for them is 60–72°F (15–22°C). Even if you live in a colder climate, you should be able to grow them in the fall and maybe even in the winter. Carrots need 1 inch (2.5 cm) of water per week when young, but as the roots mature, you can increase the water to 2 inches (5 cm) per week. You can fertilize carrots 5–6 weeks after sowing with a liquid fertilizer that is low in nitrogen and high in phosphorus and potassium. Keep the soil moist because if the soil dries out, the roots may crack, and you will get a poor harvest.

You can usually harvest carrots 60–75 days after sowing. Pull one up and see how it is when you think the time is right.

Cauliflower

Cauliflower grows best in well-drained soils with pH levels between 6.0 and 7.0.

Cauliflower is a biennial plant grown as an annual. It is best started in containers but can also be sown directly. Sow the seeds in seed starting mix ½ inch (1.2 cm) deep. Once the seedlings have germinated and plants have 3 or 4 leaves, you can transplant them to your garden beds. They need 18–24 inches (45–60 cm) of space between plants and 30–36 inches (75–90 cm) of space between rows.

Cauliflower grows best in full sun, and it needs 6–8 hours of sunlight per day. It's a cool-season crop, and it does best in moderate temperatures (60–75°F or 15–24°C). Cauliflower needs 1–2 inches (2.5–5 cm) of water per week. It needs to be fertilized a lot. You can add compost or well-rotted manure to the soil when you plant them. You'll need to add compost in mid-season as well. Alternatively, you can use a balanced liquid fertilizer once a month or according to the product's instructions.

Cauliflower is typically ready to harvest 3–4 months after planting. It's ready to be harvested when the head is fully developed. It should be 6–12 inches (15–30 cm) in diameter and still compact.

Celery

Celery prefers well-drained soils with pH levels between 5.8 and 6.8.

Celery is a biennial plant grown as an annual. It has a long growing season, so it's best to start it in containers and transplant it to your garden beds when it's ready. It's a good idea to soak celery seeds in water overnight before sowing. When the seedlings are 2 inches (5 cm) tall, transplant them into individual pots. Seedlings should be transplanted to garden beds 8 to 10 inches (20–25 cm) apart with 12–24 inches (30–60 cm) of space between rows.

Celery grows best in full sun, but it can grow in partial sun too. It needs 5–7 hours of sunlight per day. Celery is a cool-season crop that prefers temperatures between 60 and 70°F (15–21°C). Celery needs 1–2 inches (2.5–5 cm) of water per week. You can add compost at the time of planting, and then you can fertilize it with a potassium-rich liquid fertilizer every month.

When celery starts to grow, you can tie the stalks together to stop them from sprawling. You can harvest whole plants or just a stalk or two as you need them to keep the plants growing longer. The darker the stalks are, the more nutrients they contain, but darker green stalks are tougher. You can store celery in the fridge in a plastic bag for a few weeks.

When celery is ready to harvest, the stalks will typically be around 12–18 inches (30–45 cm). It usually takes 130–140 days to grow before harvesting. Harvest stalks from the outside in. You can harvest the plants whole, but cutting individual stalks will keep plants producing for a longer period of time.

Collard Greens

Collard greens prefer well-drained soil with a pH level between 6.0 and 7.5.

Collard greens are a biennial crop grown as an annual. You can start them in containers or direct sow them. Plant the seeds ¼ to ½ inch (0.6–1.2 cm) deep. Collard greens need 12–18 inches (30–45 cm) of space between plants and 18–36 (45–90 cm) inches of space between rows.

Collard greens prefer growing in full sun, but they will tolerate some shade as long as they get at least 5 hours of sunlight per day. They are a cool-season crop, and they prefer temperatures between 55 and 75°F (13–24°C). They are quite thirsty and need 2 inches (5 cm) of water per week. Collard greens don't need a lot of fertilizing—you can fertilize them every 4–6 weeks with a high-nitrogen liquid fertilizer, although a balanced fertilizer would work fine too.

Collard greens usually take 80 days to grow from seed to harvest. You can harvest the leaves as needed or harvest whole plants. Collard leaves are ready for harvest as soon as they reach usable size. You can pick a couple of outer leaves at a time—use scissors or a sharp kitchen knife to cut the leaves about an inch (2.5 cm) from where they jut out of the soil. They will be most tasty when picked young—less than 10 inches (25 cm) long and dark green. If you want to harvest the whole plant, you can cut it off above the crown if there's still some time for it to produce a few more leaves before the growing season ends. Or if the growing season is ending soon, you can pull the whole plant up and cut the roots off once it's out of the ground.

Cucumbers

Cucumbers prefer well-drained soils with pH levels between 6.0 and 7.0.

Cucumbers are annual plants. It's best to sow them directly. Seeds should be planted 1 inch (2.5 cm) deep. You can start them in containers, and they will transplant OK. Cucumbers don't like frost or cold, so don't plant them out too soon. Cucumbers need 3–5 feet (0.9–1.5 m) of space between plants if grown at ground level; however, trellised cucumbers need only 1 foot (30 cm) of space. Rows should be spaced 4–5 feet (1.2–1.5 m) for ground level plants and 1.5–2 feet (45–60 cm) for trellised plants.

Cucumbers like to grow in full sun and need 6–8 hours of sunlight per day. They are a warm-season crop that grows best in temperatures between 75 and 85°F (24–30°C). They need 1–2 inches (2.5–5 cm) of water per week. You can fertilize cucumbers every 3 weeks with a phosphorus- and potassium-rich liquid fertilizer. The main thing cucumbers need to grow well is lots of water. If you think of how much of the inside of a cucumber is water, it's no wonder that they need to be watered regularly. Don't grow cucumbers too large because they can start to taste bitter. Cucumbers can grow on a vine or on a bush. Vines tend to be more common. They have large leaves and will produce an abundant crop. You will need to have a trellis to support them. Vine varieties can grow 6–8 feet (1.8–2.4 m) tall, and bush varieties can grow 24–36 inches (60–90 cm) tall and wide.

Cucumbers typically take 55–70 days to grow from germination to harvesting. They are ready to harvest when they are bright, medium to dark green, and firm. You should avoid harvesting them when they are yellow, puffy, have sunken areas, or wrinkled tips.

Eggplants

Eggplants prefer well-drained soil with pH level between 6.0 and 7.0.

Eggplants are biennial plants grown as annuals. They are best started in containers but can be sown directly as well. Seeds should be planted ¼ to ½ inch (0.6–1.2 cm) deep. You can plant up to two seeds in each cell of a seed starting tray or sow two seeds in each hole directly. Seedlings will be ready to transplant in about 6–8 weeks. Eggplants need 18 inches (45 cm) of space between plants and 30–36 inches (75–90 cm) of space between rows.

Eggplants grow best in full sun and need 6–8 hours of sunlight per day. They are a warm-season crop that grows best in temperatures between 70 and 85°F (21–30°C). Eggplants need 1 inch (2.5 cm) of water per week. Eggplants need to be fertilized every 2 weeks with a liquid fertilizer that is high in phosphorus. You can use a balanced fertilizer too. Growing eggplants is similar to growing tomatoes. You don't need to prune eggplants, but doing so will help improve the productivity of your plants. You'll need to remove suckers when the plants are mature. You can also remove yellowing or diseased leaves and branches growing tall and lanky. Eggplant bushes can grow quite tall, so you'll need to tie your plants to a stake.

Eggplants usually take 2–3 months to grow to harvest after transplanting. Harvest eggplants with skin that is glossy and thin. Simply cut a short piece of stem above the cap attached to the top of the fruit with a sharp knife or pruners to harvest them.

Garlic

Garlic prefers well-drained soils with pH levels between 6.0 and 7.0.

Garlic is a perennial crop grown as an annual. It is grown from cloves. Gently separate cloves, and plant them at a depth of 1 inch (2.5 cm) fat end downwards, pointy end up directly in the soil. Garlic should be spaced 6 inches (15 cm) between plants and 10–12 inches (25–30 cm) between rows.

Garlic grows best in full sun, and it needs 6–8 hours of sunlight per day. Garlic is a cool-season crop, and it requires cool air temperatures of 32 to 50°F (0–10°C) during its first 2 months of growth when roots are established and bulbs begin to form. It needs 1 inch (2.5 cm) of water per week during the growing season. You can fertilize garlic in early spring with a liquid fertilizer that is high in nitrogen—blood meal is perfect for garlic. You can then fertilize it again when bulbs begin to form.

Garlic is easy to grow, and it has a long growing season. If you have purchased a hardneck (rather than softneck) variety, this will produce a flower that you should remove when it appears so that the energy can go into growing the bulb instead. If you intend to store garlic, leave it to dry for a few days in the sun before storing.

Green Beans

Green beans prefer well-drained soils with pH levels between 6.0 and 7.0. If you want to make use of vertical space, then pole beans are a good option. They can grow up fences, stakes, and other support systems. Pole beans will take longer to grow before you're able to harvest them, though. You can also get bush beans which tend to grow 18–24 inches (45–60 cm) in height, and you can usually harvest these within 2 months.

Green beans are annual plants. They don't like being transplanted, so it's best to direct sow them. Sow the seeds 1 inch (2.5 cm) deep. Bush green beans will grow 2 feet (60 cm) tall and wide, while pole beans can grow anywhere between 6 and 15 feet tall (1.8–5 m) and 2–3 feet (60–90 cm) wide. Green beans need 6 inches (15 cm) between plants and 3 feet (90 cm) of space between rows.

Green beans require full sun—they need 6–8 hours of sunlight per day. Ensure that there isn't too much shade where you plant them. Green beans are a warm-season crop that grows best when temperatures range from 65 to 85°F (18–30°C). Green beans need 1–1.5 inches (2.5–3.8 cm) of water per week. They don't need to be fertilized much. Beans enrich the soil with nitrogen themselves, so you can fertilize them with a low-nitrogen liquid fertilizer once a month during the growing season. Pole beans will need a support that is 6–8 feet (1.8–2.4 m) tall, and it's best to have the support in place before planting. Supports should be placed 3–4 feet (0.9–1.2 m) apart.

When beans are the size of a small pencil, they can be harvested, which is typically 50–55 days after planting. They are ready to harvest when the pods are 4–6 inches (10–15 cm) long and slightly firm and before the beans protrude through the skin.

Lettuce

Lettuce prefers well-drained soils with pH levels between 6.0 and 7.0.

Lettuce is an annual plant. Lettuce seeds are small and should be planted ¼ inch (6 mm) deep. I would recommend direct sowing lettuce. You can also start it in containers and transplant the seedlings to garden beds when they are 2–3 inches (5–7.5 cm) tall. Spacing will depend on the type of lettuce you're growing. Loose leaf lettuce needs 4 inches (10 cm) of space between plants and 12 inches (30 cm) of space between rows. Romaine lettuce needs 8 inches (20 cm) of space between plants and 12–18 inches (30–45 cm) of space between rows. Iceberg lettuce needs 16 inches (40 cm) of space between plants and 12–18 inches (30–45 cm) of space between rows.

Lettuce needs full or partial sun to grow and at least 5–6 hours of sunlight per day. It grows best in full sun with 8 hours of sunlight per day, though. Lettuce is a cool-season crop that prefers temperatures between 60 and 70°F (15–21°C). It's quite thirsty and will need 1.5–2 inches (3.8–5 cm) of water per week. You can fertilize lettuce every 2 weeks with a balanced liquid fertilizer. Lettuce can keep growing for quite some time—the key requirement is that it gets plenty of water. If the weather is really hot, then lettuce may want some shade in the afternoon.

Lettuce grows fairly quickly. Leaf varieties reach maturity in 30 days, but they can be harvested as soon as they reach the desired size. Other types of lettuce require 6–8 weeks to reach full harvest size. It's best to harvest lettuce in the morning and take young and tender leaves. Always take the outer leaves, and let the inner leaves grow.

Onions

Onions grow best in well-drained soils with pH levels between 6.0 and 7.0.

Onions are biennial plants grown as annuals. You can grow onions from seed or sets. Sets are essentially baby onions. Growing from sets is easier and quicker than growing from seed; however, growing from seed is not difficult. Growing from seed also allows for more choice of variety. Direct sowing onions in easier, but you can start them in containers and transplant them into garden beds later. Plant the seeds about ½ inch (1.2 cm) deep, and water them regularly. Sets should be planted 1–2 inches (2.5–5 cm) deep. Onions should be spaced 2–4 inches (5–10 cm) apart with 12–18 inches (30–45 cm) of space between rows.

Onions need full sun. Onions begin to form bulbs when a certain day length is reached. Short-day onion varieties begin to form bulbs when they receive 11 or 12 hours of daylight; intermediate-day (or day-neutral) onions need 12 to 14 hours of daylight, and long-day varieties require 14 or more hours of daylight. Onions are a cool-season crop that grows best in temperatures between 55 and 75°F (13–24°C). They need 1 inch (2.5 cm) of water per week. They need to be fertilized with a liquid fertilizer that's high in nitrogen every 2–3 weeks.

Onions need 90–100 days to grow from seed to harvest. You'll know they're ready to harvest when the leaves droop and turn yellow or brown. Gently loosen the soil around them, and then lift the onions out to harvest them. All varieties of onions will grow green stalks, and you can harvest them 3–4 weeks after planting once they reach 6–8 inches (15–20 cm) in height. Simply cut the largest outer ones, leaving at least an inch (2.5 cm) above the soil. Harvest about a third of the stalks each time.

Peas

Peas prefer well-drained soils with pH levels between 6.0 and 7.0.

Peas are annual plants. I would recommend direct sowing peas, but you can start them in containers too. Seeds should be planted 1–2 inches (2.5–5 cm) deep. You can soak your seeds in water for 24 hours before planting to speed up the germination process. Peas need 2–3 inches (5–7.5 cm) of space between plants and 18 inches (45 cm) of space between rows.

Peas can grow in partial sun, but they grow best in full sun. They need 6–8 hours of sunlight per day. Peas are a cool-season crop that grows best in temperatures between 55 and 65°F (13–18°C). They don't like temperatures over 70°F (21°C). They need 1 inch (2.5 cm) of water per week. Peas don't need lots of fertilizing. Feeding them with a balanced liquid fertilizer every 2–3 weeks is enough. Peas are natural climbers, and they need support to grow in most cases. Bush or dwarf varieties can do without support, but they won't produce a bountiful crop. Vining peas definitely need a trellis—they can grow up to 8 feet (2.4 m) tall. Bush peas can grow 18–30 (45–75 cm) tall and can also benefit from support, especially when they grow over 2 feet (60 cm) tall.

Most varieties of peas need 60–70 days to grow from planting to harvest. Harvest pea pods when they are bright green and noticeably full. They should be plump and swollen.

Peppers

Peppers prefer well-drained soils with pH levels between 6.0 and 7.0.

Peppers are perennial plants grown as annuals. They need a lot of warmth and are best started in containers; however, you can direct sow them if your greenhouse is warm enough (70–80°F or 21–27°C). For bell peppers, plant the seeds about an inch (2.5 cm) deep, and for chili peppers about ¼ inch (0.6 cm) deep. Seeds will germinate in 1–3 weeks. Transplant the seedlings to garden beds when they have at least 2 sets of true leaves. Pepper plants need to be spaced 18 inches (45 cm) apart with 30–36 inches (75–90 cm) of space between rows.

Peppers require full sun, and they need at least 6–8 hours of sunlight per day, but they will grow best with up to 12 hours of sunlight per day. Peppers are a warm-season crop that grows best in temperatures between 70 and 80°F (21–27°C). They can grow 3–6 feet (0.9–1.8 m) tall and 18–24 inches (45–60 cm) wide. They need 1–2 inches (2.5–5 cm) of water per week. Peppers need to be fertilized regularly, just like tomatoes. A liquid fertilizer with a lower nitrogen number is perfect, but a balanced fertilizer works well too, and you should use it every 2 weeks. Pepper plants can benefit from having support—stakes and cages are popular options for that. Pinching pepper plants in early stage of their growth will help them become bushier and promote growth. You can pinch pepper plants when they are at least 6 inches (15 cm) tall—simply clip the growing tip. You can also deadhead the flowers if they start appearing too early—this will help direct the plant's energy into growth.

Bell peppers take 2–3 months to be ready for harvesting after transplanting, and chili peppers can take 2–4 months to grow. You can harvest bell peppers when they're green once they reach full size and remain firm. Or you can leave them to ripen, and their color will change into red, yellow, or orange. As for chili peppers, you can harvest them once they reach their mature size and color, but the longer you leave them to ripen, the hotter they will become.

Potatoes

Potatoes prefer well-drained, slightly acidic soils with pH levels between 6 and 6.5, although they can tolerate soils with pH levels as low as 5.

Potatoes are grown from seed potatoes. A seed potato is a potato that is replanted and used to grow more potatoes. You can get them at a garden center or a nursery. Make sure to get ones that are certified and disease-free. You can cut larger seed potatoes (larger than a chicken egg) that have multiple eye buds in half to grow more potatoes. When you're cutting, make sure that each side has at least 2 sprouts. Leave them for a few days after cutting so that the wound can heal, or they will rot otherwise. You can pre-sprout seed potatoes—this will help them develop sprouts, but it's not necessary. To pre-sprout your seed potatoes, leave them in a cool, dark place for 2–3 weeks prior to planting.

Potatoes are perennial plants grown as annuals. Plant your seed potatoes 6–8 inches (15–20 cm) deep with the majority of the eyes facing upwards and spaced 1 foot (30 cm) apart. After placing the seed potatoes, cover them with soil.

Potatoes grow best in full sun. They ideally need 8 hours of sunlight per day, but they can grow in partial sun too. Potatoes are a cool-season crop, and they grow best in temperatures between 60 and 70°F (15–21°C). They need 1–2 inches of water per week. You can fertilize them with a balanced liquid fertilizer once a month.

Potatoes usually take about 3 months to grow from planting to harvest. Wait until the tops of the vines have yellowed and started to die back before harvesting them.

Radishes

Radishes prefer well-drained soil with pH level between 6.0 and 7.0.

Radishes can be either annual or biennial plants depending on the variety, but they are grown as annuals. Like with all root crops, it's best to direct sow radishes. Plant the seeds ¼ to ½ an inch (0.6–1.2 cm) deep. Radishes need to be spaced 2–3 inches (5–7.5 cm) apart with 8–12 inches (20–30 cm) of space between rows.

Radishes can grow in full or partial sun. They need at least 6 hours of sunlight per day. Radishes are a cool-season crop that grows best in temperatures between 55 and 65°F (13–18°C). They need 1 inch (2.5 cm) of water per week. Radishes don't need a lot of fertilizing, but you can use a phosphorus-rich liquid fertilizer, such as bone meal, a couple of times during the growing season.

Radishes take 20–70 days to grow from planting to harvesting depending on the variety. Early maturing varieties can be harvested in 20–40 days, while Asian radish varieties take 40–70 days to grow until harvest. A good way to tell if your radishes are ready to be harvested is to simply pull one from the soil. You can harvest them when they're about 1 inch (2.5 cm) in diameter. You can also harvest radish tops. Harvest young and green leaves, and use them in salads and soups.

Spinach

Spinach grows best in well-drained soils with pH levels between 6.5 and 7.

Spinach is an annual crop. You can start it in containers or direct sow it. Plant the seeds ½ inch (1.2 cm) deep. Spinach plants need 2–4 inches (5–10 cm) of space between plants, although some larger varieties may need 3–6 inches (7.5–15 cm) of space. Your seed packet should have information on how much space your particular variety needs. Rows need to be spaced 1 foot (30 cm) apart.

Spinach prefers full sun but can tolerate some shade. It needs at least 4 hours of sunlight per day; however, 4–6 hours is ideal. It's a cool-season crop, and it grows best in temperatures between 50 and 60°F (10–15°C). Spinach needs 1–1.5 inches (2.5–3.8 cm) of water per week. You should fertilize spinach every 2–3 weeks during the growing season with a balanced liquid fertilizer.

Spinach is usually ready for harvest in 6–10 weeks. You can harvest leaves as needed or harvest an entire plant. When the outer leaves are about 6 inches (15 cm) long, they're ready to be harvested. Simply hold each leaf with one hand, and cut the stem with the other one. Harvest no more than a third of a plant at once. If plants are near the end of the season, you can pull up or cut the entire plant.

Tomatoes

Tomatoes prefer well-drained soil with pH level between 6.0 and 6.8. Some tomatoes will grow up to 6 feet (1.8 m) tall, so you will need stakes and maybe a trellis to help grow these up. Another thing to be aware of is how many tomatoes you actually want because all the tomatoes will need to be harvested at the same time, and you'll need to be ready to use them and preserve what you don't want to use immediately. So, it's worth having plenty of mason jars if you plan to grow lots of tomatoes.

Tomatoes can be grown as perennials in their native tropical climate of South and Central America, but they are grown as annuals in other climates. Many people start with seedlings rather than seeds because they take a while to grow. If you decide to purchase seedlings, always get them from a reputable nursery. Plants should be dark green, short, stocky, and have stems the size of a pencil or thicker. They should not have yellow leaves or spots.

If you decide to grow tomatoes from seed, they are usually started in containers; however, you can direct sow them if your greenhouse if warm enough (70–85°F or 21–30°C). Plant the seeds ½ inch (1.2 cm) deep. Tomato plants need to be spaced 2–3 feet (60–90 cm) apart with 4 feet (1.2 m) of space between rows.

Tomatoes need full sun, ideally at least 8 hours of sunlight per day. Tomatoes are a warm-season crop, and they love warmth. They grow best in temperatures between 70 and 85°F (21–30°C). Tomatoes need 1–2 inches (2.5–5 cm) of water per week. They should be first fertilized when you plant them in the garden and then again when they set fruit. After tomato plants start growing fruit, you can fertilize them every 2–3 weeks until harvest. You can get a fertilizer especially formulated for tomatoes, usually with a ratio like 3-4-6 or 4-7-10. You can pinch off small stems and leaves between branches and the main stem. You can stake tomato plants, and I'd recommend doing that, as tomato plants can grow 3–10 feet (0.9–3 m) tall. You can also remove leaves from the bottom 12 inches (30 cm) of the stem.

Tomatoes can be harvested 60–100 days after planting. You can harvest them anytime they've begun to show a bit of color. Bring them indoors, and they'll ripen within a few days.

Zucchini

Zucchini prefer well-drained soils with pH levels between 6.0 and 7.5.

Zucchini are annual plants. Zucchini plants have delicate roots and can be difficult to transplant, so I would suggest direct sowing them, but you can start them in containers and transplant them later if you'd like. Plant the seeds 1 inch (2.5 cm) deep. A top tip is to plant zucchini seeds on their sides to reduce the chance of them rotting. Zucchini plants should be spaced 18–24 inches (45-60 cm) apart with 4 feet (1.2 m) of space between rows.

Zucchini grow best in full sun—they need 6–8 hours of sunlight per day. They are a warm-season crop that grows best in temperatures between 70 and 95°F (21–35°C). They need 1–2 inches (2.5–5 cm) of water per week. Zucchini don't need a lot of fertilizing. You can fertilize them once in the spring and once in the summer with a balanced liquid fertilizer. Zucchini plants can grow up to 2 feet (60 cm) tall and 2–3 feet (60–90 cm) wide. They do not necessarily need support, but they will definitely appreciate it. You can either stake them or get an A-shaped trellis.

Zucchini usually take 45–55 days to grow from seed to harvest. When you come to harvest them, remember that you can eat male zucchini flowers. You can fill and lightly batter them, but remember to leave some of these in order to pollinate female flowers. Male flowers have a long, thin stem. Female flowers have a swollen base behind the flower—this is the ovary that later develops into a zucchini after germination. When you harvest zucchini, you can cut or twist them off. Smaller zucchini are denser and have a nutty taste. Bigger zucchini are more watery, so don't be tempted to grow your zucchini to a massive size before harvesting them. They taste better when they're smaller.

Fruits

Melons

Melons grow best in well-drained soils with pH levels between 6.0 and 6.5.

Melons are annual plants. You can direct sow them or start them in containers for transplanting later on. Plant the seeds ½ to 1 inch (1.2–2.5 cm) deep. You can transplant them into garden beds when the temperatures in your greenhouse are above 65°F (18°C). Melons need 24–36 inches (60–90 cm) of space between plants and 5–6 feet (1.5–1.8 m) of space between rows.

Melons need full sun—at least 8 hours of sunlight per day. They are a warm-season crop, and they grow best in temperatures between 65 and 95°F (18–35°C). Melons need 1–2 inches (2.5–5 cm) of water per week. Melons do best when treated with fertilizer in 2 or 3 applications during the growing season. Phosphorus- and potassium-rich fertilizers are best, but a balanced fertilizer will work fine too.

Melons usually take 80–90 days to grow to maturity after transplanting. Harvest when fruits produce their characteristic melon fragrance and start to crack near the stem. A fully ripe melon will separate from the vine with light pressure. You can also cut melons from the vine with a sharp knife. Leave an inch (2.5 cm) of stem attached to the fruit to keep it from rotting if you don't plan to use the harvested melon immediately.

Strawberries

Strawberries prefer well-drained soils with pH levels between 5.5 and 6.5.

Strawberries are short-term perennials that continuously replicate and renew themselves, and they can be productive for 4–5 years, but they can also be grown as annuals that you replant each year. Strawberries are best started in containers, but you can sow them directly too. Sow the seeds thinly, and press them into the soil. They can take anywhere between 1 and 6 weeks to germinate. You can transplant the seedlings to growing beds when they have 3 sets of true leaves. Don't bury the crown when you plant them. The crown should be at the surface of the soil so that it doesn't rot. Strawberries need to be spaced 12–18 inches (30–45 cm) apart with 30 inches (75 cm) of space between rows.

Strawberries like to be grown in full sun. They need 6–8 hours of sunlight per day. They need 1–1.5 inches (2.5–3.8 cm) of water per week. You can fertilize them with a balanced fertilizer about a month after you plant them and then again a couple of months later. Established strawberries should be fertilized once a year after the final harvest.

When your strawberries bloom depends on what type of strawberry plants you've purchased. If you have got June-bearing strawberries, then you will need to harvest all the fruit in one go over 3 weeks. Everbearing strawberries will produce most of the crop in the spring and some throughout the summer and then another crop in late summer or early fall. Day-neutral varieties will produce fruit all throughout the season until the first frost. If you want a year-round supply of strawberries, then you should get day-neutral varieties. If you want bigger berries, you can consider adding a few June-bearing plants (which I absolutely love), and while you'll need to wait a year until your first harvest, they taste incredibly delicious, and it's worth the wait.

It is advisable that in the first year you pick off the flowers—this will discourage the plants from fruiting and will help focus their energy on building strong roots instead. This will help you have a bigger yield of berries the following year. If you live in a very cold area, once the strawberries have finished, you can cut the plants down to about an inch (2.5 cm) and place 4 inches (10 cm) of mulch on them. You can remove the mulch in early spring after the last frost.

Watermelons

Watermelons prefer well-drained soil with pH level between 6.0 and 7.0

Watermelons are annual plants. You can start them in containers or sow them directly. You can transplant them into garden beds when the temperatures in your greenhouse are above 65°F (18°C). Sow the seeds ½ inch (1.2 cm) deep. Watermelons need 2–3 feet (60–90 cm) of space between plants and 6 feet (1.8 m) of space between rows.

Watermelons need lots of sun—at least 8 hours per day, but ideally 10 hours. They are a warm-season crop, and they grow best in temperatures between 70 and 90°F (21–32°C). Watermelons need 1–2 inches (2.5–5 cm) of water per week. Watermelons do best when treated with a nitrogen-rich fertilizer at the start of the growing season. When flowering begins, you can switch to phosphorus- and potassium-rich fertilizer.

Watermelons usually take 70–100 days to grow to maturity from planting, depending on the variety. Harvest when the underside of a watermelon turns from a greenish white to buttery yellow or cream. You can also thump your watermelons to check if they are ready—if they sound hollow, they are ready to harvest. Cut the stem with a sharp knife close to the fruit to harvest, leaving an inch (2.5 cm) of stem attached.

Herbs

Basil

Basil likes well-drained soils with pH levels between 6.0 and 7.0.

Basil is my favorite herb, and I absolutely adore it. I love the smell, and it's so versatile—it can add such a boost of flavor to many dishes. You can get a variety of flavors of basil: sweet, purple, lemon, and Thai.

Basil is an annual herb. You can direct sow it or start it in containers. When you sow basil seeds, put them ¼ inch (0.6 cm) deep. Basil plants should be spaced 12 inches (30 cm) apart with at least 18 inches (45 cm) of space between rows.

Basil prefers to grow in full sun with 6–8 hours of sunlight per day, but it can grow in partial shade too. Basil is a warm-season crop that prefers temperatures between 50 and 85°F (10–30°C). It needs 1–1.5 inches (2.5–3.8 cm) of water per week. You can fertilize basil every 3–4 weeks with a balanced liquid fertilizer. If you know there will be a bad frost, harvest basil before this because the cold will destroy basil plants.

Basil usually takes 3–4 weeks to grow from planting to harvest. When the plants are 8 inches (20 cm) tall, they are ready to harvest. It's best to harvest basil in the morning. Picking the leaves will encourage more growth. If you don't need them immediately, you can store them to use when required by freezing or drying the leaves.

Cilantro (Coriander)

Cilantro (coriander) prefers well-drained soils with pH levels between 6.5 and 7.5.

Cilantro (coriander) is an annual herb. It doesn't like to be transplanted, so it's best to direct sow it. Plant the seeds ¼ to ½ inch (0.6–1.2 cm) deep. Cilantro (coriander) plants need to be spaced 6–8 inches (15–20 cm) apart with 12 inches (30 cm) between rows.

Cilantro (coriander) grows best in full sun with 6–8 hours of sunlight per day. It's a cool-season crop, and it grows best in temperatures between 60 and 70°F (15–21°C). It needs 1 inch (2.5 cm) of water per week, and you can fertilize it a couple of times during the growing season with a nitrogen-rich or balanced liquid fertilizer.

You can harvest the leaves when the plants are at least 6 inches (15 cm) tall, which typically occurs about a month after sowing seeds. Don't harvest more than a third of the leaves at a time. If you want to harvest seeds, you'll need to let your plants flower, which can take around 100 days from sowing seeds. To harvest seeds, leaves seed heads on your plants to dry out, and then shake them into a paper bag to release the seeds, or you can snip the entire seedhead, place it into a paper bag, put the bag in a cool, dark, well-ventilated place, and allow the seeds to finish drying in the bag for easier harvest.

Dill

Dill prefers well-drained soils with pH levels between 5.5 and 6.5.

Dill is an annual herb. It doesn't transplant well, so it's best to direct sow it. Sow the seeds ¼ inch (0.6 cm) deep. Dill plants should be spaced 10–12 inches (25–30 cm) apart with 2–3 feet (60–90 cm) of space between rows.

Dill grows best in full sun with 6–8 hours of sunlight per day. It's a cool-season crop, and it grows best in temperatures between 60 and 70°F (15–21°C). Dill needs 1 inch (2.5 cm) of water per week. It doesn't need a lot of fertilizing. A light feeding of a phosphorus-rich or balanced liquid fertilizer applied once in late spring should be enough.

Dill is usually ready for harvest 90 days after planting. To harvest, snip the stems of the leaves right where they meet the growth point on the main stem with a pair of scissors.

Oregano

Oregano prefers well-drained soils with pH levels between 6.0 and 8.0.

Oregano is a hardy perennial herb, but it prefers warmer climates. You can start oregano in containers or sow it directly. Plant the seeds ¼ inch (0.6 cm) deep. For some varieties, you don't need to cover the seeds with soil—you can simply sprinkle them on the surface of the soil. Your seed packet should have information on how deep the seeds should be planted. Oregano plants need to be spaced 12 inches (30 cm) apart with 18 inches (45 cm) of space between rows.

Oregano prefers to grow in full sun with 6–8 hours of sunlight per day. The more sun it gets, the stronger the flavor will be. It grows best in temperatures between 60 and 80°F (15–27°C). Oregano needs 1 inch (2.5 cm) of water per week. It typically doesn't need a lot of fertilizing. If you added compost to your garden beds, you won't need to do much else in terms of fertilizing. If you have a bushier plant, you can prune it once it's at least 4 inches (10 cm) tall. Pinch the top part along with the first set of leaves just above the leaf node. This will make your plant grow thick and lush.

Oregano usually takes 45 days to grow from planting to harvesting. You can start harvesting leaves as needed once the plant is at least 6 inches (15 cm) tall. Never harvest more than ⅔ of all leaves. Oregano loses flavor after flowering, so it's best to harvest it before that.

Parsley

Parsley prefers well-drained soils with pH levels between 6.0 and 7.0.

Parsley is a biennial herb grown as an annual. You can start parsley indoors or direct sow it. Soaking the seeds in water for 12–24 hours before planting can help with germination. Plant the seeds ¼ inch (0.6 cm) deep. They can be a bit finicky, so you can plant 2–3 seeds in each hole. Parsley plants need to be spaced 6–8 inches (15–20 cm) apart with rows 12–18 inches (30–45 cm) apart.

Parsley grows well in full or partial sun. It needs at least 6 hours of sunlight per day. It's a hardy herb, and it grows best in temperatures between 50 and 70°F (10–21°C). Parsley needs 1–2 inches (2.5–5 cm) of water per week. It doesn't need a lot of fertilizing. You can fertilize it every 4–6 weeks during the growing season with a balanced or phosphorus-rich liquid fertilizer. You can remove the flower stalks, and this should help the plant focus on foliage growth instead. You can also pick dead, faded, and yellowed leaves from time to time.

Parsley typically takes 70–90 days to grow from planting to harvest. You can start harvesting parsley leaves as needed 2–3 months after planting. Wait until the stems are divided into three sections before harvesting. Instead of only picking the leaves from the top, cut the entire stem carefully from the base—parsley stems are also edible and tasty.

Thyme

Thyme prefers well-drained soils with pH levels between 6.0 and 8.0.

Thyme is a perennial herb. You can grow thyme from seed or cuttings. You can start it in containers or direct sow it. Plant the seeds ¼ inch (0.6 cm) deep. Or you can save yourself the hassle of growing from seed and get a plant from a nursery and then propagate it via cuttings. Thyme plants need to be spaced 12–24 inches (30–60 cm) apart with 18–24 inches (45–60 cm) of space between rows.

Thyme prefers to grow in full sun with 6–8 hours of sunlight per day. It grows best in temperatures between 65 and 85°F (18–30°C). It's an herb that doesn't need too much water. It only needs 1 inch (2.5 cm) of water every 10–15 days. Thyme doesn't need a lot of fertilizing. You can fertilize it with a balanced liquid fertilizer every 6–8 weeks during the growing season. You can prune thyme back in the spring and summer. If you've had the plants for 3–4 years, you may want to replace them, as they may not taste as flavorful.

You can harvest thyme all year round, but to get the most flavor, harvest it just before it starts flowering. Cut only a few stems in the first year. Many gardeners don't harvest thyme in the first year at all. It's best to cut off the top 5–6 inches (12.5–15 cm) when you harvest this and do it in the morning. Don't wash it because doing so will remove the essential oils. You can freeze it or dry the leaves in the oven or by hanging them.

Flowers

Marigolds

Marigolds prefer well-drained soils with pH levels between 6.0 and 7.5.

Most marigolds are annuals, but some varieties are perennials. Most varieties of marigolds are self-seeding, so they may appear to be perennials, but in reality, they are just coming back from seed. Marigold seeds are easy to germinate, so there is really no advantage to starting them indoors. You can direct sow them when the temperatures in your greenhouse reach 65–70°F (18–21°C), and they will bloom in 8 weeks. Plant the seeds ⅛ inch (3 mm) deep. French marigolds need to be spaced 8–10 inches (20–25 cm) apart, and African marigolds need 10–12 inches (25–30 cm) of space between plants.

Marigolds are a beautiful, vibrant orange color, and they are an asset to any garden. They've been mentioned a few times in this book, and for a good reason. They are a perfect companion plant for pretty much any crop because they grow well with everything, and they help repel pests and attract pollinators and beneficial insects, such as butterflies, bees, and ladybugs.

Marigolds can grow in full or partial sun. They need 5–6 hours of sunlight per day. Marigolds grow best in temperatures between 65 and 75°F (18–24°C).

They need around 1.5 inches (3.8 cm) of water per week. They typically don't need fertilizing, especially if your soil has been enriched with compost. They typically grow 6–18 inches (15–45 cm) tall. They will bloom from late spring and until fall. You can deadhead marigolds flowers, which will make the plant look better and encourage further growth.

There is a wide variety of marigolds available all in warm, sunny colors. They can be from 6 inches (15 cm) to 4 feet (1.2 m) tall and from 6 inches (15 cm) to 2 feet (60 cm) wide. French marigolds are the most common type. There are also tall African marigolds and Signet marigolds, which are edible and can be used in salads and pastas. If you're growing the taller varieties, such as African marigolds, they may need a support stake.

Nasturtiums

Nasturtiums prefer well-drained soils with pH levels between 6.0 and 8.0.

Nasturtiums are an annual plant. They are best sown directly because they have delicate roots and don't transplant well. You can sow them directly when the temperatures in your greenhouse reach 55–65°F (13–18°C). Plant the seeds ¼ to ½ inch (0.6–1.2 cm) deep. Nasturtiums need to be spaced 10–12 inches (25–30 cm) apart with at least 12 inches (30 cm) of space between rows.

Nasturtiums do best in full sun. They need 6–8 hours of sunlight per day. Nasturtiums grow best in temperatures between 60 and 75°F (15–24°C). They need 1 inch (2.5 cm) of water per week. They don't need to be fertilized. If you fertilize them, it will increase foliage growth but won't help increase flower growth. They are fast growing and easy to look after. There are many different types of nasturtiums, including bushy plants, trailing plants, and climbers, so if you like these, you can add a variety of different types to your garden. The leaves and flowers are edible, and they have a peppery taste. Depending on the type you buy, they can be 1–10 feet (30 cm–3 m) tall, and 1–3 feet (30–90 cm) wide.

Geraniums

Geraniums prefer well-drained soils with pH levels between 6.0 and 6.5.

Geraniums come in pink, red, purple, bronze, and white. You can also get edible scented-leaf varieties. Geraniums are best started in containers, but you can sow them directly as well. They take 12–16 weeks to grow from planting to blooming. Plant the seeds ¼ inch (0.6 cm) deep. Geraniums need to be spaced 8–12 inches (20–30 cm) apart.

Geraniums need full or partial sun depending on the variety. Annual geraniums need the most sun. Geraniums are usually grown as annuals, but they can be grown as perennials in warmer climates. They grow best in temperatures between 70 and 75°F (21–24°C). They need 1 inch (2.5 cm) of water per week. You can fertilize them every 4–6 weeks with a balanced liquid fertilizer during the growing season. You can cut the plants back at the end of the growing season, and it's worth taking cuttings in case you have any losses. If you deadhead flowers, then more will grow.

My personal favorite plants to grow are tomatoes. I just think they're incredibly versatile. They're tangy, sweet, and have a rich taste. You can use them in salads, eat them as a snack, make soups out of them, and make delicious sauces for pizzas, pastas, and other dishes. But I also love the great variety of vegetables, fruits, herbs, and flowers that we grow. They all bring something to our table in terms of flavor, great nutrition, vitamins, and help us live a healthy, organic, and sustainable lifestyle.

Key takeaways from this chapter:

1. Whether buying seeds or seedlings, be certain to check all plant information thoroughly to see how big the plants grow, what sun requirements they have, what soil type they prefer, when to plant them, how deep to plant the seeds, how far apart you should space them, and when to prune them.
2. You may need to thin seedlings out to give the strongest ones room to grow.
3. Some plants, such as carrots, don't like to be transplanted, so it's best to sow them directly. Other plants can be started in containers and transplanted into gardens beds later—check this before purchasing.
4. You may need to provide support for climbing plants or plants that grow tall. You can use stakes, canes, or trellises to provide support for plants that need it.
5. Many vegetables and fruits taste better when they're smaller, so there's no need to grow them to a huge size.
6. Remember that dwarf varieties of plants are a great option if you don't have a lot of space.
7. Some berry bushes, like blueberries and raspberries, need a certain number of chill hours in order to break dormancy and produce fruit, meaning they need to spend some time in temperatures between 32 and 45°F (0–7°C). So, it's best to grow them in a separate greenhouse where you can maintain these temperatures or in containers that you can take outside.

Conclusion

Greenhouses have numerous benefits that make having one so worthwhile—they allow you to create the perfect growing environment for your plants and potentially even grow vegetables, fruits, and herbs year-round. There's nothing not to love about greenhouse gardening. I truly hope that you get as much pleasure from it as I do.

This book has covered different types of greenhouses as well as choosing the right greenhouse for your needs in Chapter 1. Chapter 2 covered planning and building your greenhouse. Chapter 3 gave detailed information about creating the perfect greenhouse environment for your plants, including adjusting temperature, humidity, and light, plus it covered what you can grow during different seasons. Chapter 4 focused on soil, including preparing garden beds as well as building raised beds. Chapter 5 looked at starting your garden, including starting plants from seed and growing seedlings as well as propagating plants from cuttings. Chapter 6 covered the necessary maintenance of your garden and greenhouse, including watering, mulching, weeding, pruning plants, providing support for plants that need it as well as cleaning and maintaining your greenhouse. Chapter 7 focused on pest control and dealing with diseases using organic options, attracting beneficial insects, and it emphasized the importance of preventing diseases from the outset. Chapter 8 looked at harvesting the bounty from your garden, looking at how you know when to harvest, how to do this safely to not damage plants, and how to store your produce to keep it fresh. Finally, Chapter 9 covered plant profiles to provide you information about the plants you might want to grow so that you have a good indication as to their sun requirements, whether they're better started in containers or sown directly, how much water they require, how often they should be fertilized, and more.

This concludes the end of this book. I think it's a really exciting topic that you can constantly work upon to improve your garden so that you can grow delicious produce to make a sustainable life for you and your family for generations to come.

I'm sure there are lots of things you can be doing, whether that's planning your greenhouse, building it, ordering seeds, starting seeds or planting out seedlings, weeding, watering, observing your garden to make sure your plants don't have any pests or diseases, or gathering your harvest. Have a wonderful time, and most importantly, enjoy it!

Resources

Types of Greenhouses

Crossley, Holly. 2022. Types of greenhouses: 6 structural styles to choose from. *Gardeningetc*. Online. 8th February 2022.

https://www.gardeningetc.com/advice/types-of-greenhouse

Deziel, Chris. 2023. 9 Types of Greenhouses. *Family Handyman*. Online. 4th July 2023. https://www.familyhandyman.com/article/types-of-greenhouses/

James, Jesse. 2024. Types of Greenhouses. *Greenhouse Emporium*. Online. 3rd February 2024.

https://greenhouseemporium.com/types-of-greenhouses/

Choosing a Greenhouse

Eartheasy. N.d. Greenhouses: How to Choose and Where to Buy. *Eartheasy*. Online.

https://learn.eartheasy.com/guides/greenhouses-how-to-choose-and-where-to-buy/

James, Jesse. 2023. How to Pick the Right Greenhouse In 5 Easy Steps. *Greenhouse Emporium*. Online. 27th July 2023.

https://greenhouseemporium.com/greenhouses-for-sale-how-to-pick-the-right-one/

RHS. N.d. Greenhouses: choosing. *RHS*. Online. https://www.rhs.org.uk/garden-features/choosing-greenhouses

Planning a Greenhouse

Arcadia Glasshouse. N.d. 10-Step Planning Guide for the Perfect Greenhouse. *Arcadia Glasshouse*. Online. https://arcadiaglasshouse.com/10-step-planning-guide-for-the-perfect-greenhouse/

Chelsea Green Publishing. N.d. 9 Things to Consider When Building Your Own Greenhouse. *Chelsea Green Publishing*. Online.

https://www.chelseagreen.com/2023/considerations-building-greenhouse/

Wisdom, Raven. 2023. 7 Things to Know Before Building a Greenhouse. *LawnStarter*. Online. 2nd October 2023.

https://www.lawnstarter.com/blog/landscaping/7-things-to-know-before-building-a-greenhouse/

Building a Greenhouse

AGF Greenhouses. N.d. Building a Foundation. AGF Greenhouses. Online.

http://www.littlegreenhouse.com/base/base.shtml

Home Depot. N.d. How to Build a Greenhouse. *Home Depot*. Online.

https://www.homedepot.com/c/ah/how-to-build-a-greenhouse/9ba683603be9fa5395fab905443ffce

James, Jesse. 2023. How to Build a Greenhouse. *Greenhouse Emporium*. Online. 21st October 2023.

https://greenhouseemporium.com/how-to-build-a-greenhouse/#greenhouse-materials-and-tools

James, Jesse. 2023. All You Need to Know About Greenhouse Foundation & Flooring. *Greenhouse Emporium*. Online. 27th July 2023.

https://greenhouseemporium.com/greenhouse-foundation/

Greenhouse Plans

Fisher, Stacy. 2024. 12 Free DIY Greenhouse Plans. *The Spruce*. Online. 2nd February 2024.

https://www.thespruce.com/free-greenhouse-plans-1357126

Mundorf, Deirdre. 2022. 12 DIY Greenhouse Plans for Gardeners on a Budget. *Bob Vila*. Online. 3rd November 2022. https://www.bobvila.com/articles/diy-greenhouse-plans/

Planet Natural. 2023. 13 Free DIY Greenhouse Plans. *Planet Natural*. Online. 8th February 2023.

https://www.planetnatural.com/diy-greenhouse/

Greenhouse Environment

Bluelab. 2023. Controlling Humidity and Temperature in Greenhouses. *Bluelab*. Online. 6th April 2023. https://blog.bluelab.com/controlling-humidity-and-temperature-in-greenhouses

Cielo. 2024. Best Greenhouse Temperature Control Techniques to Help Your Plants Thrive All-Year Round. *Cielo*. Online. 30th January 2024.

https://cielowigle.com/blog/greenhouse-temperature-control/

James, Jesse. 2023. How to Control Humidity In A Greenhouse. *Greenhouse Emporium*. Online. 27th July 2023. https://greenhouseemporium.com/control-humidity-in-greenhouse/#1-avoid-excessive-watering

Starting Garden Beds/The No-Dig Method

Garden Organic. N.d. The No-Dig Method. *Garden Organic*. Online. https://www.gardenorganic.org.uk/no-dig-method

Mitchel-Pollock, Margarita. 2021. No dig gardening: The 7 layers of a no dig garden explained. *CountryLiving*. Online. 28th August 2021. https://www.countryliving.com/uk/homes-interiors/gardens/a37393447/no-dig-gardening-method/

Raised Beds

Almanac. 2022. A Step-by-Step Guide to Building an Easy DIY Raised Garden Bed. *Almanac*. Online. 26th May 2022. https://www.almanac.com/content/how-build-raised-garden-bed

Gardener's Supply Company. 2022. The Basics: Gardening in Raised Beds. *Gardener's Supply Company*. 3rd March 2022. Online. https://www.gardeners.com/how-to/raised-bed-basics/8565.html

Margaret. 2021. How to Water Raised Beds: The Complete Guide. Online. *Crate & Basket*. https://crateandbasket.com/how-to-water-raised-beds/

Seeding and Transplanting

Collier, Sommer. 2014. Selecting Your Seeds. *A Spicy Perspective*. Online. 13th March 2014.

https://www.aspicyperspective.com/select-seeds/

Gardener's Supply Company. 2022. How to Start Seeds. *Gardener's Supply Company*. 15th February 2022. Online. https://www.gardeners.com/how-to/how-to-start-seeds/5062.html

Harlow, Ivory. 2015. How to Transplant Vegetable Seedlings. *Farm and Dairy*. Online. 15th May 2015. https://www.farmanddairy.com/top-stories/how-to-transplant-vegetable-seedlings/258509.html

Maintaining Your Garden and Greenhouse

Dawe, Jessica. 2021. Greenhouse Cleaning and Maintenance for Beginners. Online. Eartheasy. 10th October 2021.

https://learn.eartheasy.com/articles/greenhouse-cleaning-and-maintenance-for-beginners/

DripWorks. 2022. Top Greenhouse Care and Maintenance Tips. Online. *DripWorks*. 15th November 2022. https://www.dripworks.com/blog/top-greenhouse-care-and-maintenance-tips

Harrington, Jenny. N.d. Steps to Take Care of a Vegetable Garden. *SFGate*. Online.

https://homeguides.sfgate.com/steps-care-vegetable-garden-68300.html

Ianotti, Marie. 2021. How to Take Care of a Vegetable Garden. *The Spruce*. Online 14th November 2021. https://www.thespruce.com/vegetable-garden-maintenance-1403170

MacKenzi, Jill. 2018. Watering the Vegetable Garden. *University of Minnesota Extension*. Online.

https://extension.umn.edu/water-wisely-start-your-own-backyard/watering-vegetable-garden

Tilley, Nikki. 2021. Watering the Garden – Tips on How and When to Water the Garden. *Gardening Know How*. Online. 25th June 2021.

https://www.gardeningknowhow.com/garden-how-to/watering/watering-garden.htm

Weed Control

Burke, Kelly. 2022. Organic Methods for Killing Weeds Safely. *The Spruce*. Online. 16th March 2022.

https://www.thespruce.com/green-weed-killers-2152938

Muntean, Laura. 2021. How to manage garden weeds with mulch. *Agrilife Today.* 26th March 2021. Online. https://agrilifetoday.tamu.edu/2021/03/26/how-to-manage-garden-weeds-with-mulch/

Walliser, Jessica. 2017. Organic weed control tips for gardeners. *Savvy Gardening.* Online. https://savvygardening.com/organic-weed-control-tips/

Compost

Beck, Andrea. 2022. Your Step-by-Step Guide on How to Make Compost to Enrich Your Garden. *Better Homes and Gardens.* Online. 13th May 2022. https://www.bhg.com/gardening/yard/compost/how-to-compost/

Ellis, Mary Ellen. 2021. What to do With Compost – Learn About Compost Uses in the Garden. *Gardening Know How.* Online. 27th December 2021. https://www.gardeningknowhow.com/composting/basics/what-to-do-with-compost.htm

Jeanroy, Amy. 2022. How to Make Your Own Compost. *The Spruce.* Online 23rd March 2022. https://www.thespruce.com/how-to-make-compost-p2-1761841

Fertilizing

All That Grows. 2022. Organic Fertilizers: Everything You Need to Know. *All That Grows.* Online. https://www.allthatgrows.in/blogs/posts/organic-fertilizers

Cary, Bill. 2022. When and how to add organic fertilizers to your soil. *Lohud.* Online. https://eu.lohud.com/story/life/home-garden/in-the-garden/2014/05/01/add-organic-fertilizers/8578063/

Pennington. 2022. All You Need to Know About Organic Fertilizer. *Pennington.* Online. https://www.pennington.com/all-products/fertilizer/resources/what-is-organic-fertilizer

Companion Planting

Almanac. 2022. Companion Planting Guide for Vegetables. *Almanac.* 26th May 2022. https://www.almanac.com/companion-planting-guide-vegetables

Hassani, Nadia. 2021. What is Companion Planting? A Guide to Companion Planting in Your Vegetable Garden. *The Spruce.* Online. 29th November 2021. https://www.thespruce.com/companion-planting-with-chart-5025124

Hicks-Hamblin, Kristina. 2021. The Scientifically-Backed Benefits of Companion Planting. *Gardener's Path.* 29th September 2021. Online. https://gardenerspath.com/how-to/organic/benefits-companion-planting/

Pest Control

Herring, Barbara, 2018. 10 Common Garden Pests – and Natural Pesticides to Keep Them Away. *Eco Warrior Princess.* Online. 29th January 2018. https://ecowarriorprincess.net/2018/01/10-common-garden-pests-and-natural-pesticides-to-keep-them-away/

Ianotti, Marie. 2020. Companion Planting to Control the Insects in Your Garden. *The Spruce.* Online. 21st October 2020. https://www.thespruce.com/companion-planting-1402735

Johnson, Scott. 2022. Organic Pest Control for Your Garden That Really Works. Online. 4th January 2022. *Lawn Starter.* https://www.lawnstarter.com/blog/gardening-2/organic-pest-control-that-works/

Miller, Carley. 2022. 21 Companion Plants for Pest Control. *Bustling Nest.* Online. https://bustlingnest.com/companion-plants-for-pest-control/

Organic Lesson. 2018. 14 Beneficial Insects for Natural Garden Pest Control. *Organic Lesson.* 26th February 2018. Online. https://www.organiclesson.com/beneficial-insects-garden-pest-control/

Sim, Adriana. 2022. Organic Pest Control Methods for Your Vegetable Garden. *Tiny Garden Habit.* Online.

https://www.tinygardenhabit.com/organic-pest-control-methods-for-your-vegetable-garden/

Walliser, Jessica. 2017. Guide to Vegetable Garden Pests: Identification and Organic Controls. *Savvy Gardening*. Online. https://savvygardening.com/guide-to-vegetable-garden-pests/

Disease Management

Poindexter, Jennifer. 2022. Most Common Vegetable Garden Diseases and Solutions. *Clean Air Gardening*. Online.

https://www.cleanairgardening.com/most-common-vegetable-garden-diseases-and-solutions/

Smith, Cheryl. 2022. 10 Easy Steps to Prevent Common Garden Diseases [fact sheet], *University of New Hampshire*. Online.

https://extension.unh.edu/resource/10-easy-steps-prevent-common-garden-diseases-fact-sheet

The Big Greenk. 2022. 5 Common Garden Vegetable Diseases. *The Big Greenk*. Online. 1st February 2022. https://thebiggreenk.com/blog/5-common-garden-vegetable-diseases/

University of Georgia Extension. 2020. Disease Management in the Home Vegetable Garden. *University of Georgia Extension*. Online.

https://extension.uga.edu/publications/detail.html?number=C862&title=Disease%20Management%20in%20the%20Home%20Vegetable%20Garden

Vanderlinden, Colleen. 2022. Preventing Plant Diseases with Good Gardening Practices. *The Spruce*. Online. 16th May 2022.

https://www.thespruce.com/prevent-plant-diseases-in-your-garden-2539511

Attracting Beneficial Garden Insects and Pollinators

Hoffman, Fred. 2014. Plants that attract beneficial insects. *Permaculture News*. Online. 4th October 2014.

https://www.permaculturenews.org/2014/10/04/plants-attract-beneficial-insects/

Ianotti, Marie. 2022. How to Attract Bees and Other Pollinators to Your Garden. *The Spruce*. Online. 18th March 2022. https://www.thespruce.com/bee-plants-1401948

Harvesting and Storing Your Produce

Chadwick, Pat. 2020. Guidelines for Harvesting Vegetables. *Piedmont Master Gardeners*. Online.

https://piedmontmastergardeners.org/article/guidelines-for-harvesting-vegetables/

Ianotti, Marie. 2020. When and How to Harvest Garden Vegetables. *The Spruce*. Online. 17th September 2020. https://www.thespruce.com/when-to-harvest-vegetables-1403402

Poindexter, Jennifer. 2022. How to Store Your Garden Harvest Properly to Keep It Fresh Longer. *Morning Chores*. Online.

https://morningchores.com/how-to-store-your-harvest/

Tong, Cindy. 2021. Harvesting and storing home garden vegetables. *University of Minnesota Extension*. Online. https://extension.umn.edu/planting-and-growing-guides/harvesting-and-storing-home-garden-vegetables

Plant Profiles

Almanac. 2022. Growing Guides. *Almanac*. Online. https://www.almanac.com/gardening/growing-guides

Garden Design. 2022. 21 Easy Flowers for Beginners to Grow *Garden Design*. Online.

https://www.gardendesign.com/flowers/easy.html

Index

A

abutting greenhouses, 10
A-frame greenhouses, 12
air conditioning, 36
aluminum greenhouse frames, 15
anthracnose, 94
ants, 83
aphids, 82
attached greenhouses, 10
attracting beneficial insects, 91

B

Bacillus thuringiensis (Bt), 92
Bacillus thuringiensis kurstaki (Btk), 92
Bacillus thuringiensis var. san diego (Bt var. san diego), 93
bacterial diseases, 98
bacterial leaf spot, 98
bacterial soft rot, 99
basil, 125
beets (beetroot), 114
black rot, 99
black spot, 94
blight, 95
blossom-end rot, 101
broccoli, 115
building raised beds, 49
building your greenhouse, 29

C

cabbage, 115
cabbage worms, 83
carrot rust flies, 83
carrots, 115
caterpillars, 83
cauliflower, 116
celery, 116
checking and changing soil pH level, 51
choosing a greenhouse, 9
cilantro (coriander), 126
cleaning your greenhouse, 79
clear (translucent) greenhouse panels, 16
clubroot, 95
cold frames, 14
collard greens, 117
Colorado potato beetles, 84
common garden pests, 82
common plant diseases, 93
companion planting, 61
companion planting for disease management, 104
compost, 72
concrete floor, 18
concrete slab greenhouse foundation, 32
concrete wall greenhouse foundation, 31
considerations for choosing a greenhouse, 18
contact weed killers, 69
controlling greenhouse humidity, 38
controlling greenhouse light exposure, 39
controlling greenhouse temperature, 36
cooling a greenhouse, 36
crop rotation, 102
cucumber beetles, 84
cucumbers, 117
cutworms, 84

D

damping down, 36
damping off, 57, 95
deadheading plants, 76
dealing with diseases, 93
dehumidifiers, 39
diatomaceous earth, 91
dill, 126
direct sowing, 54
disease prevention, 101
downy mildew, 96
drip irrigation for garden beds, 66
drip irrigation for raised beds, 67
ductless heat pumps, 37

E

eggplants, 118
electric space heaters, 37

F

fennel, 63
fertilizing, 70

fiberglass, 16
flea beetles, 85
freestanding greenhouses, 11
fungal diseases, 93
fungicides (organic), 93

G

gable-style greenhouses, 11
gardening tools, 43
garlic, 118
geodesic dome greenhouses, 13
geraniums, 129
gothic arch greenhouses, 12
gray mold, 96
greehouse light exposure, 39
green beans, 118
greenhouse building permit, 20
greenhouse covering/glazing materials, 15
greenhouse environment, 35
greenhouse flooring, 17
greenhouse foundation, 30
greenhouse frame materials, 14
greenhouse humidity, 38
greenhouse insulation, 37
greenhouse kits, 18
greenhouse panel clarity, 16
greenhouse seasons, 40
greenhouse site preparation, 30
greenhouse temperature, 35
greenhouse ventilation, 27, 36, 39
grow lights, 28, 40
grow lights for starting seeds, 56
growing seedlings, 57

H

hand pollination, 78
hand weeding, 69
harvest, 106
heating a greenhouse, 28, 37, 39
homemade organic fertilizers, 71
homemade organic fungicides, 93
homemade organic pesticides, 89
hoop houses (Quonset style), 13
hydronic heating systems, 38

I

insecticidal soap, 90
intercropping, 61
issues with seeds, 56

L

lacewings, 92
ladybugs, 92
last frost date, 54
leaf miners, 85
lean-to greenhouses, 10
lettuce, 119

M

maintaining your garden, 74
maintaining your greenhouse, 79
making compost, 73
marigolds, 62, 128
maximizing growing space, 61
mealybugs, 85
melons, 124
Mexican bean beetles, 86
misting/fogging system, 36
mosaic virus, 100
mulching, 67

N

nasturtiums, 62, 128
neem oil, 89
no-dig gardening, 45

O

onions, 119
opaque (diffused) greenhouse panels, 16
oregano, 126
organic fertilizers, 70
organic seeds, 53

P

parsley, 127
peas, 120
peppers, 120
pest control, 89
pesticides (organic), 89
pill bugs, 86
pinching plants, 76
planning your greenhouse, 23
plant families, 102
plant growth stages, 74
plant profiles, 114
plastic greenhouse frames, 15
pollination, 77
polycarbonate, 16
polyethylene film, 16
potatoes, 121

potting up seedlings, 58
powdery mildew, 97
preparing garden beds, 45
propagating plants from cuttings, 60
pruning plants, 76

R

radishes, 122
raised beds, 48
root-knot nematodes, 86
rust, 97

S

seed starting mix, 55
seeding and transplanting, 53
selecting and starting seeds, 53
semi-opaque greenhouse panels, 16
shade cloths, 36, 40
shading, 40
shallow hoeing, 69
slugs, 86
snails, 86
soil floor, 17
soil pH level, 51
spider mites, 87
spinach, 122
springtails, 87
squash bugs, 87
starting no-dig garden beds, 46
starting seeds in containers, 54
steel greenhouse frames, 15
stone/gravel floor, 18
storage conditions for vegetables and fruits, 110
storing your harvest, 110
strawberries, 124
support for tall or vining plants, 77

T

tempered glass, 15
thermal mass, 37
thrips, 88
thyme, 127
tobacco hornworms, 88
tobacco mosaic virus, 100
tomato hornworms, 88
tomato spotted wilt Virus, 101
tomatoes, 122
transplanting seedlings, 59
types of greenhouse materials, 14
types of greenhouses, 9

V

verticillium wilt, 98
vine weevils, 88
viral diseases, 100

W

watering garden beds, 65
watering raised beds, 67
watermelons, 125
weeding, 69
wet wall, 37
whiteflies, 88
wooden greenhouse foundation, 30
wooden greenhouse frames, 15

Z

zucchini, 123

Printed in Great Britain
by Amazon